The Calculating Passion
of Ada Byron

[JOAN BAUM]

The Calculating Passion
of Ada Byron

Archon Books
1986

First published 1986 as an Archon Book,
an imprint of The Shoe String Press, Inc.,
Hamden, Connecticut 06514

Printed in the United States of America

The paper in this book meets the guidelines
for permanence and durability of the
Committee on Production Guidelines for Book Longevity
of the Council on Library Resources.

Library of Congress Cataloging-in-Publication Data

Baum, Joan, 1937–
The calculating passion of Ada Byron.

Bibliography: p.
Includes index.
1. Lovelace, Ada King, Countess of, 1815–1852.
2. Mathematicians—Great Britain—Biography.
3. Calculators—History.   4. Computers—History.
I. Title.
QA29.L72B38   1986   510'.92'4 [B]   86-14103
ISBN 0-208-02119-1 (alk. paper)

To
Sidney & Sonia

[CONTENTS]

[ACKNOWLEDGMENTS]

Although the emphasis here is on Ada Lovelace and Charles Babbage's Analytical Engine, anyone writing on Byron's daughter owes an inestimable debt to Doris Langley Moore for her full and fascinating account of Ada's personal life (1977). And for anyone interested in British science and technology in the first half of the nineteenth century, Anthony Hyman's fine 1982 study of Babbage is also necessary reading. Needless—but a delight—to say, I am grateful for having had as a reader of some sections Peter Hilton, Distinguished Professor of Mathematics at the State University of New York at Binghamton.

No research can proceed with relative ease without the aid of extraordinary librarians, and Lovelace scholars are blessed in Mary Clapinson, Senior Assistant Librarian in the Department of Western Manuscripts, at the Bodleian Library, Oxford. My thanks to her, to her assistant Colin Harris, and to staff in the Science and Technology Room at the New York Public Library. To Mihai W. Handrea, Donald H. Reiman, and Robert Yampolsky, of The Carl H. Pforzheimer Library of New York, and to Robert Machalow, of the York College Library, I also want to express appreciation for their knowledge and good humor.

Of course, I am indebted also to the owners of the Lovelace and Somerville papers and to their representatives for permission to read and to publish: To the Earl of Lytton, owner of the Lovelace Papers, and his agents, Laurence Pollinger Ltd., and to the Hon. Lady Fairfax-Lucy, owner of the Somerville Collection, and her representative, Gordon L'E. Turner, Senior Assistant

Curator at the Museum of the History of Science at Oxford. Thanks also to Marjorie G. Wynne, at the Beinecke Rare Book and Manuscript Library, at Yale University, for permission to quote from a letter of Mary Somerville to Ada Lovelace, and to curators of the Bodleian Library for permission to quote from Ms. Acland dep. 22. Again, I am grateful to Doris Langley Moore and to her publisher, John Murray, for permission to reproduce illustrations.

Many who answered persistent inquiries will find themselves in the bibliography. Others, including Tsu-Chih Wu, Jeff Mc-Gowan, and Frederic Baum, will, I hope, recognize the fruits of their suggestions.

Although it is considered good form to thank one's editor, I do so here with authentic pleasure. In a publishing world that has become increasingly impersonal, I consider myself lucky in having The Shoe String Press family as associates.

Finally, very special thanks to four York College colleagues and friends: George Dorris and Rainer Pineas, of the Department of English, for their careful reading and caustic comments; Joseph Malkevitch, of the Department of Mathematics, for his meticulous intelligence and good-natured sufferance of all my questionings; and most of all Alan Cooper, chairman of the Department of English at York, for his wise, critical, and imaginative review of this work in all its stages. What errors and infelicities remain are mine alone.

[CHRONOLOGY]

January 2, 1815:
Anne Isabelle (Annabella) Milbanke, daughter of Sir Ralph and Lady Noel, marries George Gordon Byron, sixth Baron Byron.

December 10, 1815:
Augusta Ada Byron is born at 13 Piccadilly Terrace, London.

January 1816:
Lady Byron leaves her husband.

April 24, 1816:
Deed of separation is signed: Byron leaves England for good.

April 1817:
Ada is declared a Ward in Chancery.

April 19, 1824
Byron dies at Missolonghi, in western Greece, and is refused burial in Westminster Abbey.

June 5, 1833:
Ada meets Charles Baggage: two weeks later she sees the Difference Engine in his Dorset studio.

November 1834:
Ada sees plans for the Analytical Engine; shortly after, she attends lectures on the Difference Engine given by Dionysius Lardner.

July 8, 1835:
Ada Byron marries William King, eighth Baron King, at Fordhook, Lady Byron's residence.

May 12, 1836:
Ada gives birth to first child, Byron Noel King. In 1838 Byron is given courtesy title of Viscount Ockham and becomes Baron Wentworth on the death of Lady Byron in 1860.

September 22, 1837:

Ada give birth to second child, Anne Isabelle Noel King, who becomes Lady Anne Blunt, upon marriage.

June 30, 1838:

Ada King becomes countess of Lovelace when William is created first earl of Lovelace.

July 2, 1839:

Ada gives birth to last child, Ralph Gordon Noel King. Ralph takes the surname of Milbanke instead of King, in 1861, and becomes Baron Wentworth, in 1862, upon the death of his older brother. Upon his father's death, in 1893, he becomes second earl of Lovelace. The Lovelace line continues through him.

February 1843:

Ada begins translating Menabrea's article on the Analytical Engine and adds "Notes."

August 1843:

Translation and "Notes" are published in Taylor's *Scientific Memoirs.*

November 27, 1852:

Ada dies after an agonizing bout with cancer and is buried in the Byron vault at Hucknall Torkard, near Newstead Abbey, the Byron ancestral home in Nottinghamshire.

Overview: The Lady and the Engine

The eminent—and eccentric—nineteenth-century mathematician Charles Babbage (1791–1871) begins his autobiographical *Passages from the Life of a Philosopher* (1864) with an unintentionally ironic recollection: when he was young, his mother often took him to exhibitions of machinery. At one, a man called Merlin took the fascinated young boy to his attic workshop to show him "more wonderful automata." These turned out to be two silver female figures about twelve inches high: graceful, in exquisite mechanical motion. One walked or glided; the other danced "with a bird on the forefinger of her right hand, which wagged its tail, flapped its wings and opened its beak." This "admirable danseuse," Babbage recalls, "attitudinized in a most fascinating manner." Her eyes were "full of imagination, and irresistible." The "chef-d'oeuvres" of their artist, the figures must have required "years of unwearied labour, and were not even then finished." And so the memory concludes, and Babbage moves on to recall other boyhood incidents. Little did the child realize that the dancer would reappear many years later in both real and symbolic form.

Quite by accident, during the summer of 1834, at an auction of a mechanical exhibition, Babbage, now forty-three, rediscovered his Silver Lady. Delighted, he bought her for £35, put her back in working condition, and installed her in his London salon alongside his Difference Engine, an automatic calculating machine he had constructed with government support. The Silver Lady turned on rotating pegged cylinder barrels, the very mechanism Babbage had been considering for another invention, an Analytical Engine. Visitors to his studio that year were delighted with the Silver Lady, but one of them was more fascinated by the Difference Engine. She was Ada Byron, a slim, elegant, dark-haired girl of nineteen, slightly withdrawn, fond of dancing, sometimes called by her mother "the bird." The daughter of Lord Byron, the poet whose affairs—and poetry— had recently scandalized the nation, she had come again to see Babbage's famous calculating engine and now the drawings for his new machine. Fragile, like his silver mechanism, this admirable lady, "full of imagination, and irresistible," captivated Charles Babbage. Long after her own irreparable mechanism would fail, because of cancer, Babbage would still owe to her the best interpretation of his Analytical Engine, the world's first computer. Later on, she would be hailed by many as the first to write a complex set of instructions, or "illustrations," for that engine—the world's first computer "program." She would also be the first to publish speculations about what an engine like the one Babbage was envisoning might do.[1] It is for those speculations, perhaps even more than for her mathematical illustrations, that she is primarily remembered.

Recognition came late. For one hundred years after her death there was silence, and then, in 1952, tribute in a book on the history of computing.[2] And now, only in the last few years, there has been a rush of information—books, articles, excerpts from her letters, with more on the way. Here was a remarkable lady, overlooked in the history of science, a Victorian woman working presciently in a man's field. And here was what she did over the course of a few months in 1843: She not only wrote "Notes," which envisioned and explained a "program" for Babbage's Analytical Engine and were the first sophisticated sequence of coded instructions ever written for such a mechanism; she also anticipated computer developments such as artificial intelligence and computer music. The actual "program," a means to generate a complicated sequence in the calculus known as the Bernouilli numbers, was an ingenious choice to prove the necessity for and the power of Babbage's great machine. Ada had understood the uniqueness of Babbage's plans for an engine that would control itself internally, make choices, and retain partial results in a memory set for final calculations. She had also dared to dream, to imagine what computers might do with their power to repeat and loop and change course in midstream. And she had exercised her imagination when time and place were against her, when women were excluded from the halls of learning and generally dissuaded from pursuing subjects like mathematics, even in the drawing rooms. The "Notes" were a particularly remarkable feat, since in fact no Analytical Engine ever was built. Ada's imagination had been fired only by Babbage's drawings and plans.

How is it then that Augusta Ada Byron King, Countess of Lovelace, should intuit so much about computers one hundred years before their time, yet remain merely a footnote to the history of mathematics? It is tempting to invoke the biases of times past and of recorded history and say that Ada Lovelace has been lost amidst studies of Byron, Babbage, and the history of ideas; that youth, gender, social position, and illness required her to keep aloof from Victorian high society and to assert her intellect anonymously. It is tempting, even, to call her Ada and thereby unintentionally diminish her—she was always known as Byron's child, and she was young when she met Babbage, young, still, when she died in 1852, shortly before her thirty-seventh birthday. Indeed, it might be said that Lady Lovelace has been passed over in the history of mathematics because women intellectuals in the nineteenth century too often have been ignored; that she would have accomplished more in mathematics had illness not claimed her; that she is remembered only as Babbage's "interpret*ress*" because she died too soon. All this might be said, but it should not be all. To account for Ada Lovelace's limited achievement, these are necessary conditions, but not sufficient ones. Her story is more instructive than a feminist cliché.

Mathematically talented, Ada Lovelace joined skill with benevolence to help Charles Babbage explain inventions his country failed to comprehend. Then, when the twentieth century reclaimed Babbage as the father of mechanized digital computing, his dazzling light eclipsed her own faint shining. But what Ada Lovelace did in annotating a translation of notes on Charles Babbage's Analytical Engine was important to the appreciation of plans for the world's first computer. Although questions remain about the substantiveness of her contribution in the history of mathematics and about the constancy of her mathematical intentions,[3] the U.S. Department of Defense in 1980 named its new programming language "Ada" after her.

Though not an original theorizer or inventor of a system, Ada Lovelace was apparently a fine mathematical expositor, described as such by historians of science, such as Lord B. V. Bowden, who rediscovered her "Notes" in 1952, and by Babbage himself, who, charmed as he was by her, was no fool. Theirs was a deep and abiding friendship—no more than that—but Babbage was no base flatterer. He was impressed by her energy and her accomplishment. Essentially, however, Ada Lovelace claims attention not because Victorian science needs its record amended but because she was indeed the world's first computer "programmer" and for a long time the best appreciator of Babbage's Analytical Engine, the most remarkable and misunderstood invention of its time. She was also Byron's daughter and, just as significantly, Lady Byron's. The mother's blood may have determined her mathematical course; the father's may have diverted it.

At a crucial time in her life Ada Lovelace felt, and acted on, a "power" and a "passion" to go far in mathematical pursuits. That she even entertained such notions was unusual; that she went as far as she did—studying continually, corresponding with leading mathematicians, and publishing a commentary in a leading science journal of the time—could be regarded as radical. But Ada Lovelace did not soar against the prevailing winds of Victorian society. It was childhood conditioning—and inheritance—that moved her, not social rebellion. Indeed, if being a woman might have restricted her, social class could compensate. Lady Lovelace was the wife of a very supportive husband, an earl,[4] and enjoyed the advantages of being married well. In her time, although women did not compete equally with men, a lady of her station could expect certain rules to be eased. In 1834, for example, the year Ada saw the plans for Babbage's contemplated Analytical Engine, the British Association for the Advancement of Science discovered the benefit of having the fair sex in attendance. Upper-class women were not summarily excluded from the halls of science, since, as modern historians note, "considerations of sex and style led back to questions of aristocracy, of patronage, and of the purse."[5] Moreover, records show how woefully behind the times Cambridge was. The system and curriculum of Britain's leading university would only have impeded a progress Lady Lovelace was free to make by virtue of family and class. For Ada, the daughter of a lady very much used to getting her own way, doors to study could be opened. If Ada did not open them, it was for reasons that had more to do with inner turmoil than with the temper of the times. In the very period when she was preparing the "Notes," and afterward, when it would have seemed most natural for her to go into newer and higher mathematical spheres, there was already at work the pull of fame and of its perverse counterpart, infamy.

Although her work is slight—the "Notes" constitute no more than forty pages and were her sole publication—Ada Lovelace's claims on our attention are considerable. Her story reflects subjects of contemporary interest: the education of women in the first half of the nineteenth century; concern about science writing; the history of computers; the arguments of nature and nurture in assessing talent; and the effects of illness on intellectual intentions and achievement. Not least, Ada engages us because she was the child of one of literature's most fascinating figures. It was Byron, not Babbage or Bernouilli, who was in her blood.

Said to be courteous, sociable, and charming, Ada Lovelace could also seem strange, reclusive, and moody. The anatomist Henry Acland, who went riding with her one afternoon in 1839, found her blunt and so "very curious" that he amused himself in thinking she might be a "Papist" or a "witch," and told her so.[6] He was not the only one to wonder about her. Byron's best friend, John Cam Hobhouse, who saw Ada occasionally at dinner parties, commented on her eccentricity. At one gathering, she was "rather fantastic," though amiable and interesting; at another, a dinner guest "in a whisper" asked if she "was not mad."[7] Foolish rumors, Hobhouse concluded, but his record of them testifies to their currency.

In 1841, some months before she started to write on Babbage's Analytical Engine, Ada sent a prospectus on her future, a kind of mathematical manifesto, to her friend Woronzow Greig, son of the famous mathematician Mary Fairfax Somerville and the best friend of William King, now Lord Lovelace. The prospectus prompted Greig to reply with some praise but more anxiety. He acknowledged Ada's "peculiar development of extraordinary powers," unusual in one so young and differing "entirely not only from powers of your own rank and condition but from the generality of mankind."[8] But he also spotted restlessness, and a certain ambition to become as famous as her father, whose memory had been so ambivalently preserved by Lady Byron. Greig told her that the name she would hand down to her own children might be "even more distinguished" than that which she had received "from her ancestry," but he urged her to tread the path to glory cautiously. She had been "cradled in celebrity," he affectionately lectured her; "haunted by" might be the more accurate term. A Byronic fire was fanning passions in Lady Lovelace that mathematical training had been intended to repress or cool.

When Ada Byron was married at the age of nineteen, the *World of Fashion* reported that the "fair," "highly accomplished," and "most amiable" young heiress had obviously realized the prayer breathed by the departed poet: "she has escaped the dangers and woes which enclosed her footsteps, the clouds that gathered round the morn of her life. . . ."[9] The notice was tragically premature. Too soon, Lady Lovelace would be "classed / With forms which live and suffer," as her father had written in his autobiographical poem, *Childe Harold's Pilgrimage*.[10] Ada herself, as she lay dying, elected a line from his dramatic poem *Cain:* "Believe—and sink not! doubt and perish,"[11] an apparently unwitting embroidering of the family motto, *Crede Byron*. It would seem that the melodramatic Childe Harold may have had a child, though Lady Byron would not have been pleased to think so. Her main motive in urging mathematics on Ada had been to prevent "Byronic" influence. Shortly after Ada's death, Lady Byron gave her grandson Ralph, Ada's youngest child, an 1853 edition of *Childe Harold* with the dedication: "Along in the Poetry, study the Philosophy, but mistrust the Personality."[12] What she did not say was that she had failed, finally, to inculcate this lesson in Ada.

Ada Lovelace's life might easily be viewed as an extension of Lady Byron's. Determined after the notorious separation from her husband to make Ada exclusively her own, Lady Byron initiated a war against her husband in the courts which was continued in the public domain and pursued, after his death, and even hers, by partisans on both sides. Byron had not been reformed, her side argued; marriage had not redeemed him. He had had an affair with his sister, took drugs and drink, had fits of insanity, liked boys—this last charge, which Lady Byron had heard about, was perhaps the most offensive in homophobic Regency England.[13] Central to Lady Byron's plan was her wish that Ada be disciplined by mathematics. Ironically, however, it was Ada's intense but short-lived activity on behalf of Babbage's Analytical Engine that most showed her to be, after all, Byron's child—restless, passionate, fanciful.

Ada's recognition of her own Byronic impulses came late—too late, perhaps, to effect a resolution of inner conflict. The "Notes," written in a burst of concentrated energy and revisionary thrall, did not attract much attention, and Ada did not press on. She had hoped for fame, enough to rival her father. She would achieve only minor notice among those in her circle, and limited celebrity later on as Babbage's assistant. To acknowledge this fact, however, is not to diminish her. Quite the contrary. Lady Lovelace was a young woman of enormous intellectual energy and ambition, whose mathematical story deepens the Byron legend by illustrating the tragic consequences of forcing native talent to symbolic purpose.

[CHAPTER 1]

The Programming
of Ada Byron

She called them "Notes," which is what they really are—
seven brief technical essays on Babbage's Analytical Engine,
forty slight pages, considered now to be the world's first explanation of computer programming. The science editor and publisher Richard Taylor brought them out in 1843 as part of his
Scientific Memoirs series (1837–1852), translations from the transactions of foreign academies of science. In 1840, Babbage had
lectured in Turin on the concept of an analytical engine. An
Italian engineer, Luigi Federico Menabrea, who had heard him,
wrote up a "Sketch" of the engine, which appeared in 1842, in
French.[1] One year later, Ada's translation was published, ac-
companied by "Notes." These, in type smaller than that of the
articles themselves, were the last entry in the volume.

Almost one hundred and fifty years after their publication,
Alan Turing, famous as the code breaker of the Government
Code and Cypher School, at Bletchley Park, referred to Ada's
"prophetic insight,"[2] and Babbage's most recent biographer,
Anthony Hyman,[3] called her interpretation of the Analytical
Engine a remarkable achievement. Charles Babbage knew that.
He called Ada Lovelace a better expositor than he of his own
ideas, "intimately acquainted" with "almost all the very difficult
and abstract questions connected with the . . . [Analytical
Engine],"[4] and he urged her to publish the work separately,
under her own name. What had started out as a translation of
Menabrea's "Sketch" on the "executive" features of Babbage's

1

new machine developed into an extensive commentary on programming—the first of its kind. Of course, Ada did not use "programming," a word that came into use only in the 1940s, when the concept was quite advanced, but she did anticipate many of its ideas—or interpret and illustrate them.

When Bowden rediscovered Ada's "Notes" and reprinted them in 1953, he called them "the first comprehensive account of Babbage's engines . . . [he] had read."[5] It was the first time most people had heard of Ada Lovelace and her annotation of Babbage's computing machine. Although Bowden's was not the first reprinting of the "Notes," it was the critical one. In 1889, one of Babbage's sons, Maj. Gen. Henry Prevost Babbage, had included the "Notes" in a collection of papers and articles on the Analytical Engine, but not until the computer revolution got under way a half century later did the "Notes" attract attention, and only after Bowden's book came out did Ada herself begin to emerge from obscurity. New music of the spheres had been sounded the year Ada's "Notes" were published, but there were only a few then who heard its complex melodies, who knew that among the first to understand how a machine might appear to think and follow complicated rules for calculation was a twenty-eight-year-old countess whose very interest in mathematics had been largely a "programming" to remove her from the shadow of her notorious father. Indeed, many in Ada's circle knew little about her mathematical interests, and fewer still were acquainted with her work. Trained in arithmetic and algebra but never pursuing them with consistent or exclusive energy, Ada seemed to have just "happened upon" the notion of writing on Babbage's Analytical Engine, while apparently remaining indifferent to many scientific discoveries of the day. A certain reticence was understandable, however, since Victorian ladies did not readily overstep intellectual boundaries, particularly in the mathematical sciences. So a certain modesty prevailed, and the author of the "Notes" was identified only as A.A.L. But with the publication of the "Notes" in 1843 in Taylor's third volume,[6] computer programming can be said to have begun.

It was the "software," to risk an anachronism, that Ada concentrated on, not the machine—what the engine could be made to do, rather than how it might be constructed. As a matter of fact, Babbage's Analytical Engine was conceived as mechanical, to run on steam. Although someone in the second half of the nineteenth century did work on an electrified version of the Jacquard loom that furnished Babbage with "programming" ideas, Babbage did not incorporate electricity into his plans. Moreover, the engine was designed for the decimal, not the binary, system.[7] It is ironic that Babbage called his invention a "calculating" engine; "computer" then was the more restrictive term, standing for a counting device that only did arithmetic, or for a person whose job it was to add up figures. Ada appreciated the significance of the different terms.

But even if she, his "Enchantress of Number," had written extensively on his engines, as he had urged, nothing much would have changed for her, or for him. After the "Notes" were published, Ada said she was eager to get involved in having the engine built, but she was eager to get involved in other scientific projects as well, and with other advisers. Babbage would have gone on tinkering in any case, and technology would still have been slow to accommodate itself to his plans: a hundred years later, when the world's finest Electronic Numerical Integrator and Calculator (ENIAC) was built, indirectly incorporating some of Babbage's ideas, it was 100 feet long, 10 feet high, 3 feet deep, and ridiculously expensive[8]—no improvement in this regard on Babbage's own projected monster. As Ada no doubt knew, however, from talks with Babbage, size and sluggish engineering skills were not the invention's only impediments. In fact, Allan Bromley, the Babbage scholar who examined recently discovered engine plans, has argued persuasively that the Analytical Engine could have been built with the technology at Babbage's disposal.[9] The formidable problem lay elsewhere.

Unlike Babbage's earlier machine, the Difference Engine, a model for which had won supporters in 1822, the more complex Analytical Engine, which never moved beyond plans, defied general understanding. Scientists and political leaders who might have provided funding were also put off by Babbage's sometimes caustic manner. What if Ada had gone more into society and promoted his ideas? Lord Melbourne (William Lamb, 1779–1848), who was prime minister in 1834 and from 1935 to 1841—critical years for Babbage—was Lady Byron's first cousin. Then again, Lady Melbourne, Lord Melbourne's mother, had been Lord Byron's confidante, reason enough to antagonize Lady Byron. But Lord Melbourne's wife, Lady Caroline Lamb, was reason even more for Ada to keep away, for Caroline had not only chased after Byron quite openly, she had also written about her escapades and published a thinly disguised fiction about the man who was "mad, bad, and dangerous to know"—to the delight of Regency society.[10]

Ironically, it was Lord Lovelace, more than Ada, who seemed to press for Babbage in the great world. Lovelace was genuinely fond of the great inventor and approved of the friendship with his wife. Lovelace was also ambitious, having acceded to the earldom only recently. It would have pleased him, probably, had Ada actively sought to promote Babbage's machines. She was one of the Victorian period's aristocratic scientific ladies, amateurs who loved and pursued the disciplines of natural philosophy. Bluestockings, many of them, they were the female counterparts of the "Gentlemen of Science" who professed faith in a benevolent bond between knowledge and class. Patrons of literary and philanthropic associations, and diarists of the intellectual endeavors of their time, these women interested themselves in education and science with an earnestness suggestive of the felt obligations of their class. Seen against such a background, however, Ada seemed peculiar, in an eccentric orbit all her own. In 1842, the year Menabrea's article on Babbage's Analytical Engine appeared on the Continent, Hobhouse recorded in his *Diary* for May 19 that Ada's manner and talk were "not those of a woman of the world." She was a young woman of enormous but often unfocused intellectual energy, and the exercise of talent may have been for her less the required expression of Victorian service than an outlet of personal need. In any case, the countess of Lovelace could not be counted on to advance Babbage's engine with the influential members of her class.

But even if she had been active on Babbage's behalf, by 1842, the year she would begin writing the "Notes," her advocacy would have come too late.[11] That very year Sir Robert Peel, himself a mathematician, decided that the government had had enough of Charles Babbage's engines, maybe even enough of

Babbage.[12] The brilliant inventor was a perfectionist, constantly revising, while great reserves of money were spent (his own as well as the government's) and perhaps even greater reserves of patience. The earlier machine, the Difference Engine, which was expected to generate nautical tables, was still not completed. The chancellor of the exchequer, Henry Goulburn, was finally fed up. Mockingly, Peel suggested in the House of Commons that Babbage's Difference Engine should be set to calculate the time at which it would be of use.[13] As for the Analytical Engine (always in the planning stage), that was mistakenly assumed to be just another version of the earlier invention.

By the time Babbage died, in 1871, he had been at work on the Analytical Engine (and on publishing accounts of his quarrels with Parliament) for almost forty years without ever completing a working model. Ada chided him about his habits, though with affection: finish your "tit-tat-to" game, she wrote in a chatty note in 1848; *complete* something!"[14] He did, of course—scores of books and pamphlets, reviews and articles, drawings and mechanisms of various kinds—but by late 1842, the Analytical Engine, his ultimate dream, was turning into a nightmare. Ada, who teasingly suggested she was his inspirational "fairy," may have been one of the very few to know that Babbage wore the crown of a mythical kingdom, for the truth was that Babbage realized early on that he could never complete an efficient working Analytical Engine that would incorporate all the powers he foresaw for it. For the time being, plans would have to be sufficient. Charles Babbage had genius and he certainly had charm, but he also had quirks, including a passion to rid England of organ-grinders, who had robbed him, he said, of nearly one-fourth his thinking time. He was twenty-three years Ada's senior, but they got along splendidly. Lady Lovelace had passions and oddities of her own.

She was observed at different times by different people to be diffident, bold, ironic, shy, arrogant, charming, willful, submissive—apparent contradictions that seemed to feed the curiosity she aroused from the day she was born. It was not easy being known as Byron's daughter. Though some childhood letters bear the signature "AAda," her first name, Augusta, for Byron's half-sister, was not used after 1816, when rumors of incest about Byron and his half-sister, now Mrs. Augusta Leigh, grew rife. Lady Byron was convinced (or said she was) that Medora Leigh, Augusta's child, had been fathered by Byron and not by Augusta's husband, Col. George Leigh. Byron was wicked, Byron was wild, Lady Byron had argued in the courts, hinting at more. Byron, however, wrote as though Ada had always been his daughter's only name: "It is short—antient—vocalic" and had been in the Byron family for years, not to mention the Bible; Lameth's wife in Genesis is named Ada, he pointed out.[15] Byron also recalled Charlemagne's sister and the commonality of the name in the days of King John. "A-da" had also been the future Lady Byron's (Annabella Milbanke then) playful form of "adieu" in their courting days. Byron's dwelling on small details is noticeable and sad. In self-imposed exile from the time of the separation in 1816 until his death eight years later, he somehow knew he would never see his "little Da" again.[16] He also knew that hypocritical British society enjoyed tales of scandal.

By the time she came to write the "Notes," Augusta Ada Byron King, countess of Lovelace, had been married for eight years and had three children, but she was known only to a small coterie as a student of mathematics. To the world she would continue to be known as Ada Byron—a designation which sometimes bothered her. Charles Dickens, for example, in 1843 found himself apologizing. He was, he wrote, "too well assured of the interest felt by Lady Lovelace in all that concerns the improvement and happiness of the people, to have ever entertained the idea of addressing her . . . *merely* as the daughter of Lord Byron."[17] Henry Acland, however, must have been living in another world, for in 1839, after he had gone riding in the countryside with the "curious" Lady Lovelace, he wrote that he had only recently discovered that she was Byron's daughter. At the very least, his ignorance shows that Ada then was not emphasizing the fact. But people knew. The *Examiner*'s editor, Albany Fonblanque (1793–1872), a frequent visitor to the Lovelace home, put the matter aptly: "Who has not felt an interest in the only child of Byron, the Ada whose name is so caressed in his verse, and a lock of whose hair is the subject of a touching passage in his letters? Who has not felt at least a curiosity to know what features of genius and character had descended from the father to the daughter?"[18]

Although an 1848 article in the *Atheneum* identified the countess of Lovelace as the translator of Menabrea's "Sketch" of the Analytical Engine and the author of the "Notes," the reference was brief and insufficient to replace the heritage with the achievement. What is more, Ada would soon begin to be known as Byron's "legitimate" daughter: Little Allegra, Byron's child by Shelley's sister-in-law, Claire Claremont, died in Italy at the age of five, so there was truth as well as genuine emotion in the impassioned cry of Byron's protagonist, Childe Harold: "ADA! Sole daughter of my house and heart" (Canto III; 1816). From afar, from the time of the separation until his death in 1824, Byron worried about his child, continually asking for news. She was often ill, he heard. What would he have felt had he been alive when she was reported suffering from a paralytic disorder at fourteen and forced to go on crutches for a while? By chance, Ada would be treated then by Dr. Henry Herbert Southey, brother of the poet laureate, Robert Southey, whom Byron had mocked in his satiric verse epic *Don Juan* and even more mercilessly in the shorter satire *The Vision of Judgment* (1822).

There were enough periods of health and energy, however, to support Doris Langley Moore's suggestion that many of Ada's youthful illnesses may have been neurasthenic. She liked the outdoors. In one of her most charming notes, she wrote Babbage in January 1841 that he must come for a visit, for mathematical conversation, of course, but she also urged him to dress warmly and bring ice skates. Like Byron, Ada also loved horses and riding, passions she shared with her husband. Toward the end of her life, however, her love of horses got disastrously confused with gambling, though the full disaster will never be known, since damaging letters about bookmakers and debts, suspicious gaps in an otherwise complete correspondence, are no longer available. Regardless, it is difficult not to sense in Ada's increasingly erratic behavior, beginning shortly before the composition of the "Notes," the impress of her mother, the "hen," sometimes more like a vulture, feeding on the reputation of the errant Lord Byron. Ada's childhood seems to have been for Lady Byron an arena in which she contested for her daughter's soul.

Although embryologists knew better, it was generally believed then that only males influenced life and that women were merely childbearers, an assumption about character rather than physical resemblance.[19] What Byron saw in a miniature portrait of his "little girl" convinced him that she resembled her mother, except for the mouth. But as to "little Ada's" occasional outbursts of "violent" temper, which he had heard about from Augusta, these, he wrote his publisher and friend, John Murray, were no surprise, considering the mother—a "sullen nucleus of concentred [sic] Savageness."[20] Byron obviously believed in the power of nurture over nature ("contagion" was his word for the Milbanke household). Lady Byron may also have believed in nurture, however, because she felt there was something in heredity that she needed to act against—and could, she thought, through mathematics. Her husband, she kept telling lawyers and allies, was both mad and bad.

Looking back on Ada's younger days, Sophia Frend De Morgan (1809–1892), eldest daughter of Ada's one-time tutor William Frend, remarked that it was "very evident" that Ada Byron "inherited many of her father's peculiarities" and "tendencies," and that had it not been for Lady Byron's "careful training," Ada's heedlessness, imprudence, vanity, prevarication, and conceit might never have been modified. Although one could not make a "Newton into a Mozart—a Dr. Johnson into Raffaelle," Sophia went on in her memoirs, "in the early part of this century, and in the good old times that were before, it was the general belief . . . that teaching will form character. No matter from what parents a child is born, give him but suitable training, and you may make what you please of him."[21]so Lady Byron argued about education in general and about her own child in particular.

She drove her daughter hard, and this at a time when even intellectuals sympathetic to the study of mathematics by women believed that women were constitutionally not as fit for abstruse learning as men. Ada does not seem to have considered the matter one way or the other, though in an 1844 letter to Sophia about recent "past derangements," she indicates that one cause among others of a recent illness was *"too much Mathematics."* She apologizes, through Sophia, to Augustus De Morgan, the mathematician, now Sophia's husband: ". . . I have been *utterly unable to think* even of my Studies. I yesterday resumed them; but for some time I must only give them ½ an hour to an hour a day. Pray tell Mr. De Morgan all this; he must wonder at not having heard from me." But the implication was that he would hear from her soon, as she hoped she would soon have "at least *something* [mathematical] to trouble him with."[22] De Morgan had met Ada shortly before his marriage in 1837, when he began to advise her in mathematics. Sophia, who revered the virtuous Lady Byron but was never too fond of the daughter, may even have felt that Ada's "past derangements" had an obvious genetic cause. What is more likely, however—to borrow a theme from Coleridge in "Dejection, An Ode"—is that that which suited a part infected the whole. Ada had been depressed, had sought consolation in mathematics, but had overdone it. Three years earlier, when her mother had written a disclosure letter about Byron's incestuous affair with Augusta, Ada was devastated to the point of intellectual paralysis. It was one of the few periods in her life when even mathematics was suspended for a while, and then invoked for tranquil restoration. Ada had been educated, after all, to use mathematics as a control for too-passionate emotions.

Mathematics was first for Lady Byron a mode of moral discipline. Accordingly, she arranged a full study schedule for her child, emphasizing music and arithmetic—music to be put to purposes of social service, arithmetic to train the mind. She herself, so William Frend had said, had been a talented student of mathematics; it was both natural and desirable, therefore, that she foster the right kind of learning in her child, her sole care. Interestingly, however, Ada Byron was not at first attracted to the subject or compelled by its discipline. According to a Miss Lamont, one of an ever-changing guard of Lady Byron subordinates, Ada's favorite subject was geography. Miss Lamont's journal portrays a dutiful six-year-old doing arithmetic with no particular enthusiasm but a desire to please her mother.[23] An entry for June 6, 1821, indicates that little Ada found arithmetic the least agreeable of her lessons, a difficulty

Lady Byron met by substituting a lesson in numbers for one in geography and, in July, by substituting for Miss Lamont, who was let go. Miss Lamont was not the only one to keep a journal of Ada's progress, however. Lady Byron kept one for the same period, copying down Ada's words for her future edification. The first entry, June 1, 1821, begins ominously: "I, Ada, have not done the Notes very well, but I'll try to do it better tomorrow. . . . I was not pleased with myself at all—. . . ." The last entry, in April, is no more sanguine: "I've not been so good. . . . I shall try to be better." Significantly, the word was "be," not "do."

Lady Byron's education of Ada turned on rewards and punishments, the latter including solitary confinement, lying still, and written apology. Lessons ranged, with breaks, from morning until after dinner, but study might be extended if lessons were not done "with alacrity and docility." Miss Lamont reported, for example, that little Ada had an ability to add up "sums of five or six rows of figures, with accuracy" and was usually "deliberate and correct," but when she got tired and sloppy, Miss Lamont officially recorded, Ada had to make amends by doing everything again. The picture that emerges is of a very bright adult-child (an only child who, when not with grown-ups, was almost always alone) who can spell difficult words of one or two syllables; knows the definition of "noun" and the divisions of the earth; can draw parallel lines with a pencil; and "can explain the words parallel, perpendicular, horizontal."[24]

Augusta, not yet fully ensnared in Lady Byron's biased accounts against her wicked husband (who was now burning up the Continent with cantos of the autobiographical *Don Juan*), wondered whether Ada was not being pushed too much. So did Byron. There had been earlier concern about Lady Byron's many absences, what with the separation and Lady Byron's various benevolent activities. Even Lady Noel, Lady Byron's mother, hinted that Annabella might spend more time with her child.[25] Byron sarcastically expressed the same wish directly to his estranged wife: "They tell me young Pip is well & shews marvellous indications of acquaintance with her nurse & her Grandmother:—it is perhaps time that she should begin to recognize another of her relations."[26] But if Byron had worried that a sometimes absent mother meant an absence of watchfulness and involvement, he was very wrong.

Lady Byron was determined to design a rational universe for her child, even instructing governesses to avoid mentioning "ghosts" and other such fanciful notions. Years later, if Ada had heard Babbage's delightful accounts of childhood conjuring, tales which would find their way into his autobiography, how unlike her own childhood his must have appeared. Lady Byron notwithstanding, in time her daughter, the future writer of the "Notes," would on occasion associate herself with the "Devil" as she worked. She also expressed interest in studying scientific deduction by way of the black arts and the effects of poison, as she wrote Agnes Greig, Woronzow Greig's wife, in February 1841. Only three months earlier, Ada had written to her mother one gloomy afternoon that she would like to be reading something on the connections between evil and the horrible, between supernatural powers and knowledge.[27] The expression was more fitful than Byronic, but it was hardly calculated to put Lady Byron at ease.

Little did Byron realize how much his daughter would resemble him despite their different intellectual talents—though on occasion Ada could write sentimental and derivative poetry whose saving grace would be its infrequency. "Ada is very fond of mathematics, astronomy and music but possesses no soul for poetry" was the observation of the bluestocking Caroline Fox in her *Memories of Old Friends*,[28] an observation that would seem to grant Byron's own dramatic wish: "I hope the gods have made her anything save *poetical*."[29] They did, and in a way that would have pleased him, though not Lady Byron. With what mixed sentiments she must have written to Ada from Germany in 1838 about an amusing conversation she had overheard at a restaurant, about a "swarthy" Lady Byron who never smiled and her child, "very fond of accounts—what a thing for a Poet's daughter!"[30] Lady Byron seems to have fancied herself serving both muses, with a decided preference, in poetry, for the didactic. Ada's talents, however, would clearly lie elsewhere, or so the mother determined.

It was phrenology that confirmed for Lady Byron her daughter's intellectual abilities, though Sophia and Lady Byron did find it puzzling that Ada's head "showed imagination, wonder, constructiveness and harmony, with very high intellectual powers"—configurations that suggested the "making of a poet." In fact, however, as Sophia attested in her memoirs, little Ada winced at the reading of her father's poetry, thinking the words of a popular song quite as good. It did not take both ladies long to resolve the apparent difficulty: "Language was not so powerful as the . . . [other forces]; had it been so, there would probably have been a musical poetess instead of, or perhaps as well as, a cultivated poetical musician. As has been often noticed in other cases, music and mathematics were indicated in the head, and were both strong elements of character.'[31] Harriet Martineau, a contemporary bluestocking of more sense and substance than Caroline Fox, wrote in her *Autobiography*, "such empirical practice [phrenology] is insulting and injurious to true science,"[32] but Lady Byron did not see it that way. She believed in the practice and consulted phrenologists frequently, Ada sometimes in tow. Caroline Fox records a telling incident:

> Saw the—Foxes. They are very full of Deville, the phrenologist, with whom they have had some intercourse. He told them of an anonymous Lady whom he had to caution against sensitiveness to the opinion of others. Some years afterwards she came again and brought a daughter, who, when finished, was sent into another room, and the lady consulted him upon her own cranium. He found the sensitiveness so fearfully increased as almost to require medical treatment. He afterwards met her at a party, when she introduced herself to him as Lady Byron.

That Lady Byron's "sensitiveness to the opinion of others" was often occasioned by something to do with Byron can be seen in Caroline Fox's mention of a "third visit" to the famous phrenologist. It was "whilst [Thomas] Moore's *[Letters and Journals* of Lord Byron, with notice of his] Life . . ." was being published [1830], and, in accordance with his prescription, Lady Byron had not allowed herself to read it"—so she said.[33]

Ada was under influence of Lady Byron all her life and, despite occasional rumblings, close to her until the end. Yet certain Byronic qualities did not escape the notice of the observant Fonblanque: "She was thoroughly original," he wrote in a brief memoir after her death, but had one trait, a "poetic temperament," in common with her father."[34] What only intimates would have known, however, was that Ada could be at times more Byronic than Byron. She could write confidentially and confidently to Greig in February 1845, ". . . neither matrimony nor anything else in the world *can* come up to the *ideal* of an imagination like mine, which is powerful & vivid." She sounded at times like her father's sentimental hero Childe Harold, unable or unwilling to invoke the satirizing ironies of his later self-reflecting hero, Don Juan.

Though Byron was not to know it, because he died when his daughter was only eight years old, Ada would develop a significant interest in a discipline that for Lady Byron would remain only superficial. Byron was on the right (ottava rima) track in *Don Juan* when he ran over his wife's intellectual pretensions in the character of Donna Inez: "Her favourite science was the mathematical, / Her noblest virtue was her magnanimity, / Her wit (she sometimes tried at wit) was Attic all, / Her serious sayings darkened to sublimity" (I, xii). It was a doubly damning line, since Byron makes Donna Inez Juan's mother, not wife, and "a walking calculation," whose "thoughts were theorems" (I, xiii). The image obviously appealed to Byron, since at the time he was composing the canto, he used the same words in a letter to his good friend Thomas Moore. The innocuous part had begun, "I have a great love for my little Ada, though perhaps she may torture me like. . . ." The rest of the remark, which Moore had censored, continued: ". . . the mathematical Medea, her mother, who thinks theorems and speaks problems; and has destroyed, as far as in her lay, her husband, by only shaking her head. . . ."[35] There could be no doubt who was intended to get the satiric arrows in *Don Juan:*

> 'Tis pity learned virgins ever wed
> With persons of no sort of education,
> For Gentlemen, who, though well born and bred,
> Grow tired of scientific conversation.
> I don't choose to say much upon this head,
> I'm a plain man, and in a single station,

But—Oh! ye Lords of ladies intellectual,
Inform us truly, have they not hen-pecked
   you all?

(I, xxii)

Before his marriage, Byron had playfully referred to his future wife as "the Princess of Parallelograms," unaware of the deadly seriousness of his description: ". . . her proceedings are quite rectangular, or rather we are two parallel lines prolonged to infinity side by side but never to meet." Directly, to his betrothed, he would innocently continue the banter:

> I agree with you quite upon Mathematics too—and must be content to admire them at an incomprehensible distance—always adding them to the catalogue of my regrets—I know that two and two make four—& should be glad to prove it too if I could—though I must say if by any sort of process I could convert 2 & 2 into *five* it would give me much greater pleasure.—The only part I remember which gave me much delight were those theorems (is that the word?) in which after ringing the changes upon A-B & C-D etc. I at last came to "which is absurd—which is impossible" and at this point I have always arrived & I fear always shall through life. . . .[36]

The truth is that Lady Byron, supreme in matters of self-glorification, was more interested in mathematics as a means than an end. Ada, on the other hand, had a real "passion" for numbers, one that she said had to be "gratified." The lava of imagination belonged to both father and child; the bedrock of vigilance, to the mother.

Passion, vagaries, play—these were dangers to be guarded against with the right kind of education. In a letter typical of her moral posturing, Lady Byron wrote a cohort that one of her "sins and misdemeanors" was a "fancy" that Ada's youthful imagination could be led astray "by the poetical colouring of circumstances"—this, when Ada was just over two years old. However, Lady Byron was prepared to act on that notion: "Be this as it may," she declared to her confidante, "I ought to provide against the contingency by every means in my power." She tried. "The greatest defect" in Ada, she wrote her old ally, Dr. William King (1786–1865), whom she engaged as tutor when

Ada was thirteen, is "want of order—for this the Mathematical science would perhaps form the best remedy." She outlined a course of study for King to follow with Ada, beginning with arithmetic and algebra. Two weeks later she expressed her pleasure that King had "commenced . . . [his] operation on Ada's brain."[37] But there were others in reserve: a Miss Arabella Lawrence was employed shortly after and urged to use her Unitarian ways to curb Ada's argumentative disposition. A part of King's "operation on Ada's brain" obviously took, however. Years later, shortly before she was to begin composition of the "Notes," Ada wrote her mother that it was a "very strange thing, that so disorderly as I generally am about papers & such things, there is yet never any disorder in any part of my mathematical papers or proceedings. This is a curious phenomenon!"[38]

From the beginning of her studies, when Ada was just five, Lady Byron had insisted on the cultivation of mathematics primarily because its discipline represented for her the direct opposite of everything associated with her depraved husband: dangerous fancy, melancholy moods, evil, even insanity. Yet for all Lady Byron's desire to dominate, Ada did eventually seek tutors and mathematical correspondents on her own. The most significant, of course, was Charles Babbage, to whom she attached herself with insistent but Platonic devotion.

Ada began writing seriously to Babbage about mathematics four months before she gave birth for the first time. She would later on refer to the "Notes" as her "child" and her "uncommonly fine baby." The time was January 1836; Ada was twenty-one, pregnant, no longer moving in society. But she was not exactly resting throughout her confinement, either. Babbage had been sending her puzzles, but it was mathematics she mainly wanted to talk about. She's been getting on "delightfully" with Lardner's *Trigonometry*, she writes, which, as far as she had gone, she thinks "excellent," and she notes, with a girlish enthusiasm determined to impress, that a great deal of paper has been destroyed in working out "quantities of formulae."[39] It is conceivable that Charles Babbage was a father figure for Ada and she a substitute for the daughter (approximately Ada's age) he had lost in the autumn of 1834 and for the sons who did not share his intellectual curiosity. Even so, Ada chose carefully someone to whom she could entrust her heart as well as her head. Their letters to one another show a side of Ada that marks her in the Byron line: witty, playful, ironic, fated.

Lord Lovelace was often mentioned in Ada's letters to Babbage, and on occasion Lovelace himself would write to the famous inventor, urging him to visit, though the invitation was usually on behalf of his wife, who wanted to discuss mathematics. Eleven years older than Ada, socially correct, a bit reserved, William, eighth Baron King, who became first earl of Lovelace in 1838, three years after his marriage to Ada, and lord lieutenant of Surrey one year after that, was proud of his wife and supported her mathematical endeavors, even to the point of helping her copy parts of the "Notes." Lady Byron was delighted with the match: William King, already high on the social ladder when he married his nineteen-year-old heiress, was exactly what Lady Byron had wanted in a son-in-law—someone proper, someone pliant. He must have been less than memorable, however. In his *Recollections,* Hobhouse writes that in 1840, when Lord Lovelace was sworn in, at the palace, he had "never seen him, although he was the husband of Ada Byron."[40] Letters show that there was more discussion of significant domestic matters between mother and son-in-law than between husband and wife or mother and daughter, though in fairness to Lady Byron it should be said that Ada did not seem to mind. The "hen," as Lady Byron called herself (to Ada's "thrush" or "bird" and William's "crow"), liked to be in control. Her daughter's intellectual pursuit of Babbage (though he was an old acquaintance of Lady Byron) would be one of the few courses she would not direct. William King, however, was quite manageable—and naïve. "What different constitutions you and Lady Byron have," he wrote his would-be bride the summer of their marriage. "But this may be owing to her [Lady Byron's] more delicate state of health."[41] The valetudinarian Lady Byron lived to be sixty-eight years old, almost twice the age of her daughter. There were many aspects about the Byrons that Lord Lovelace did not see, not least among them what mathematics meant to Lady Lovelace.

[CHAPTER 2]

The Mathematical
Milieu

Three years before Ada was born, the effects of two separate events, one political, the other mathematical, merged in a way that would change life dramatically in England, though not many in the second decade of the nineteenth century would have suspected it. On February 27, 1812, less than one month before the sensational publication of the first two cantos of *Childe Harold*, the still obscure Lord Byron made his maiden speech in the House of Lords: an impassioned plea on behalf of the frame-breakers and against a bill that would make frame-breaking a capital offense. In 1811, beginning in Nottinghamshire, Byron's own district, Luddites—reportedly so named after a mythical Ned (King) Ludd, said to be a Leicestershire weaver—banded together to protest recently introduced stocking and lace frame-machines; wages were low, job losses were feared, and riots ensued. In 1812, Luddites were fired upon by soldiers, killed, hanged, or transported. Their cause, as much as the harsh reaction to the protests, became a Whig rallying cry. Byron, it has been said, was one of the few members of Parliament who looked primarily to the cause, not the crime, of Luddism.

Meanwhile, a little more than a hundred miles away, at the university of Cambridge, a quieter kind of revolt was beginning, the applications of which would eventually benefit the middle and working classes, though at first just the opposite would seem true. The event was the formation of the Cambridge

Analytical Society, essentially the brainchild of its three most prominent members, all Trinity men: the algebraist George Peacock (1791–1858), the astronomer John Herschel (1792–1871), and the mathematician Charles Babbage (1792–1871), the last of whom would look to a weaver, Joseph Marie Jacquard (1752–1834), for the punched-card principle of the Analytical Engine—cards with holes specifically punched, allowing threads to be woven in certain patterns.[1] Jacquard had constructed an automatic drawloom in 1801, and Babbage would have a portrait of himself woven on it in brocaded silk. The well-known historian of mathematics Carl Boyer refers to this period from 1812 to 1815 as "the turning point in British mathematics."[2] In fact, the period was one of several involving Babbage that would later be understood as important in British mathematics: 1822 marked the completion of Babbage's first model for the Difference Engine; 1832, the Oxford meeting of the British Association for the Advancement of Science, indicating the association's "emerging centrist character";[3] 1842, Menabrea's "Sketch" of the Analytical Engine; 1852, the Report of a royal commission of inquiry on the need for curricular and administrative reform at Cambridge University. Babbage's calculating engines, along with Ada's "Notes," would reflect new mathematical emphases, but the engines themselves would have no direct influence on the development of computers or programming, a fact that recalls the baleful influence politics can have on intellectual endeavor.

As politically liberal as Cambridge was at the turn of the century, its mathematics curriculum was conservative. With few exceptions, the colleges were still held captive by the memory of the genius of the place, Leibniz's great rival, Sir Isaac Newton. In effect, Newtonian emphasis meant that Cambridge, England's leading mathematical university, and particularly Trinity, the largest college, were behind the times: dominated by Euclidean geometry; dedicated to Newton's dot system of notation for the calculus, as against Leibniz's use of dy / dx, a mathematically more informative and flexible system of notation; and slow to adopt developments from abroad, especially from Paris, home of materialism and godless rationalism. Patriotism alone, particularly for some years after the French Revolution, would have militated against Britain's being receptive to intellectual ideas from France. At the turn of the century, Cambridge mathematical life was still classical and essentially competitive. Euclidean geometry and Newtonian optics and astronomy were measures of deductive reasoning and confirmations of God; Senate House examinations in mathematics were confirmations of careers; and only honors in the mathematical examinations, the mathematical "tripos," led to an honors degree—a situation that would not change until mid-century.[4]

Despite a curriculum weighted in favor of mathematics, Cambridge in the early decades of the nineteenth century was committed to educating gentlemen in the liberal arts, not to training mathematicians. There was no such profession then, professions being understood to be in law, theology, or the military. Most of the Fellows of the Royal Society, the oldest scientific establishment in England, had little mathematical experience or primary interest in the natural sciences, but even if they had, it would not be until 1851 that tripos examinations would be established for the natural and moral sciences. In 1841 Lord Lovelace got himself elected to the Royal Society—not, however, because he was primarily curious about natural philosophy (though he was indeed interested in architecture, engineering, and agricultural matters), but because such membership was advantageous, he felt, to an aspiring career. He may also have wanted to accommodate his wife, who was urging him to get books for her from the society's library.[5] (Still, Ada would suggest that Woronzow Greig sneak her into the research division—shades of Caroline Lamb disguised as a boy to visit Byron!)

Cambridge then was not associated with research mathematicians. The great men of English science and mathematics at the time—John Dalton, Thomas Young, Michael Faraday, Humphry Davy, George Boole, and Babbage—were not based at the university when they did their important work. Cambridge was mainly for the awarding of degrees to prospective members of the Anglican clergy, many of whom would subsequently be employed as teachers. But the university prepared for even this goal haphazardly, to judge from contemporary accounts of debt, debauchery, and "moral turpitude."[6] A more serious problem was the felt tyranny of the mathematical tripos, which relied on the prescribed curriculum and by means of which careers were made or broken. In 1844, assessing Ada's talents, Augustus De Morgan (1806–1871) concluded that she would have been "an original mathematical investigator, perhaps of first-rate eminence," but not, he suggested, if she had gone to the university (had it admitted women then), where the system would have demanded sacrifice of originality. Perhaps De Morgan was projecting: he himself had done well on the tripos but not spectacularly.

Across the Channel it was a different story: mathematics was enjoying a golden time. The technical École Polytechnique, established in 1795, was the most formidable institution of its kind, attracting leading savants, among them Adrien Marie Legendre, Gaspard Monge, Jean Baptiste Biot, Sylvestre François Lacroix, Pierre Simon Laplace, Joseph Louis Lagrange, Lazare Carnot. The problem was that their works were unavailable for the most part in England. Only in Scotland, where Mary Fairfax Somerville, the nineteenth century's best-known woman scientist, grew up, was French analysis easily accessible, owing no doubt to the presence there of prisoners of war who had trained at the École Polytechnique,[7] and also to the "auld alliance" between Scotland and France which dated to the thirteenth century. And only on the Continent, largely at institutions not connected with the universities, was a practical kind of mathematics officially addressed. Exceptions in Britain during the last decade of the eighteenth century were few. One was the self-taught John Dawson (1734–1820), who lived in the remote Yorkshire village of Sedbergh and who from 1781 to 1794 lectured on Continental analysis (the calculus and theory of functions).[8] It was probably types like Dawson who tutored north-country grammar school boys like Wordsworth, generally to send them on to Cambridge, with fine mathematical preparation, at least one year ahead of competitors. Dawsons, however, were rare, both in the grammar schools outside the north country and at the universities. In 1808, the *Edinburgh Review* noted that a poor state of mathematical science put Britain at a disadvantage. Coincidentally, it was this same year that Byron, then a student at Trinity, mocked the domination of Euclid in a magazine devoted to Cambridge wit.

By contrast, French mathematicians in the late eighteenth century had been spurred by military demands to invent new systems and notation and encouraged to apply their talents to commerce and industry. A significant effect of French attention to applications was the work of the great civil engineer Gaspard François de Prony, who in the late 1790s prepared extensive trigonometric and logarithmic tables for the Republic by separating workers into three divisions: those who decided on formulas, those who applied them numerically, and those who did the actual computations. The idea of division of labor had been taken from an Englishman, Adam Smith, whose *Wealth of Nations* (1776) de Prony had chanced upon. But the English took it back as a promissory note, so to speak, when Babbage, who had visited de Prony in 1819, wrote about the idea in *On the Economy of Machinery and Manufactures* (1832) and adapted it for the Difference Engine, whose operating principle, the method of finite differences, was (as Hyman notes) the mechanical analogue of de Prony's system. Babbage saw that any task requiring precision and repetition, such as the generation of mathematical tables, could be done better by machine than by human computers.[9] Though Babbage was unusual for his time in advocating theory joined with application, official funding for his Difference Engine was an acknowledgment by the government of the need for accurate and efficient tables. Indeed, until 1835, a typical British scientist with 140 volumes of arithmetic and trigonometric tables in his library could expect in a forty-volume sample to have over 3700 errors; even the errata table contained mistakes.[10]

In Britain at that time, mathematics tended to be either "pure" or "applied," and, when applied, associated with theoretical physics rather than with mechanics or engineering. Indeed, from the Renaissance on through the eighteenth century, the word *engineer* carried a pejorative connotation, suggesting one who contrived, designed, or invented in order to lay snares and foment evil. Satan was often referred to as an "engineer." Because an engineer usually designed military devices rather than public works (it was an "enginer" whom Hamlet would have "hoist with his own petar"), the word probably retained some negative meaning into the 1830s, a great period of civil engineering, when it was used to describe one who constructed roads, canals, harbors, and drainage works—technical knowledge not addressed in the universities.

Turing's biographer, Andrew Hodges, himself a Cambridge mathematician, writes that even by the 1930s the situation had not changed significantly, "there being in English universities no tradition of combining high academic status with practical benefits." In the 1820s, when Babbage wanted to study advanced construction techniques and workshop conditions, he had had to go abroad, and when he proposed that meetings of the British Association be held at nonuniversity towns in order to encourage links between those towns and the universities, his suggestions were not acted upon. In vain did he recommend the contemporaneous study of mathematics, mechanics, and manufacture, an interconnection of science, engineering, and political economy. But only among a few outstanding British military and naval officers could such a union of natural philosophy and technology then be found. Behind Babbage's "growl" of frustration over his engines, which his good friend John Herschel noted often characterized Babbage pronouncements in the 1830s, there was an accurate picture of British science as an enterprise in isolation and decline.[12] Babbage truly believed he was alone, and the first to experiment with sophisticated calculating machines. In fact, as historians of science now know, he was only the first to publish the basic idea of a difference engine.[13] But if not alone, he was certainly philosophically in the minority.

As Ada knew, Babbage's perspective on the useful was a mathematician's, and one of the earliest themes enunciated in the "Notes" is the inadvisability of construing the word *useful* in too narrow a manner. The distinction is emphasized in the first note, which contrasts the different purposes of Babbage's two machines, the Difference Engine and the Analytical Engine. By 1843 the Difference Engine, though no longer supported by the government as a project, had been accepted in principle as a useful device to calculate tables by addition and to generate output. Although the Analytical Engine, still in plans, was also designed to calculate, using all four arithmetic functions, its main value would be apparent only to mathematicians. Taking up the cause of the latter machine, Ada argued in "Note A" that

"Those who incline to very strictly utilitarian views" slight the advantages that come from "abstract and speculative science . . . ," and might misunderstand the definition of *"useful"* as only that which "bears upon every-day and human interests. . . ." The "useful," she declared, could also be interpreted as advancing the nature of the discipline, a theme Babbage had sounded thirty-one years earlier. By 1843, however, Parliament had discontinued its generous subsidies of the "useful" machine and had thrown up its hands in ignorance and impatience over plans for the more conceptual one. Nonetheless, some of Babbage's ideas, if not the principles of the engines, eventually took hold at the university.

Dedicated to the immodest goal of making mathematics at Cambridge professional and leaving the world "wiser than they found it," Babbage's short-lived but influential Analyfical Society was established in 1812 to promote "d-ism," as opposed to the "dot-age" of the university, Babbage punningly declared— "d's" representing the Leibniz notation in the differential calculus (where dots signified the old-fashioned Newtonian notation) and "d-ism" referring not only to mathematical notation but to "deism." In 1830, Babbage would link both concerns, mathematical and theological, in his *Ninth Bridgewater Treatise,* which Ada read and questioned him about as she was composing the "Notes." There were, in fact, only eight Bridgewater treatises, works commissioned by the Royal Society, in accordance with the will of the earl of Bridgewater, to argue from scientific evidence for the existence of God. Babbage wrote his own account, numbering himself into the series as number nine.[14] What particularly interested Ada in Babbage's *Treatise* was his argument that miracles are merely the illustrations of a higher law set on the mechanism of the universe. Just so, Babbage had concluded, an artist might contrive an engine to obey any given law, including preordained, rare exceptions, and then revert to familiar laws; this apparent aberration would appear to the user of such an engine as "miraculous." It would also, of course, suggest something godlike about the inventor of such an engine.

In general, however, the Cambridge "Analyticals" of the early decades of the nineteenth century were out to reform mathematics, not religion. Babbage had arrived at Cambridge in 1810 with knowledge both deep and wide, his schooling, untypically, having included practical studies in astronomy, navigation, and mechanical arts. It was navigation texts that also taught the new mathematics to Mary Fairfax (later Mrs. Somerville). French mathematics textbooks had been hard to come by, but Babbage got hold of them. In *Passages*, Babbage complained that Lacroix's *Elementary Treatise on the Differential and Integral Calculus* (1816), which he translated with Herschel and Peacock, was dismissed at Cambridge because it would not be on the examinations. Indeed, in the early part of the nineteenth century, it was even possible at Cambridge to become senior "wrangler" (highest debater and therefore winner of highest honors) without ever acquiring a knowledge of the differential calculus. It was only in 1820, after the Analyticals wrote *Examples to the Differential and Integral Calculus* (part III, *Examples of the Solutions of Functional Equations*, was done by Babbage, with the new notation), that the Analyticals' movement to import Continental mathematics began to take hold. Twenty-three years later, as she was writing the "Notes," Ada asked Babbage to send on the *Examples* which she needed, she said, in order to follow the theory of the engine.

The problem of an adequate mathematics curriculum was part of wider intellectual problems at Cambridge. In *Passages*, Babbage noted that he knew more than his Trinity tutors, which was true, but he also felt unable to outdo his friend Herschel on the tripos, and so he did not read for honors. Then again, when Babbage was elected to Cambridge's highest chair in mathematics, the Lucasian professorship (he served from 1828 to 1839), he—who knew so much about Continental mathematics—gave no lectures, nor was he obligated to do so. Cambridge, in short, did not engage its best minds either in research or in teaching. Moreover, some of the most prominent academics did not always meet their responsibilities: The story was told of the philosopher William Whewell, who was angered when finally told that one of his students had been dead for months.[15]

Important work often went on elsewhere because there was no real scientific community at the universities and little government support of mathematical or scientific ideas. "Eccentric" might well describe many of the best British men of science and mathematics then. They worked alone, not in common enterprise, and they tended to work on a single idea or point of view, reflecting no school of thought or philosophy.[16] Mary Shelley's *Frankenstein* accurately reflects the frustrations of a natural philosopher who wants to "banish disease from the human frame, and render man invulnerable to any but a violent death!" (chapter 2). But Frankenstein was a solitary; like Babbage, he constructed his own instruments and followed his own unappreciated fancy. Frankenstein created a "monster," not because he lacked morality or intelligence (benevolent motives are the heart of the novel) but because he lacked technical expertise. The University of Ingoldstadt had not furnished him with a stimulating intellectual community. Nor would Cambridge when *Frankenstein* was published in 1820. The curriculum there would not change for another thirty years, despite the development in the 1830s of an intellectual network, a "loose convergence of scientists, historians, dons, and other scholars" who wanted to share ideas on science and theology.[17] They occasionally met at scientific meetings later on in the decade, but they were appreciators for the most part, writers, teachers, translators, and natural philosophers whose bond was more liberal Anglicanism than focused mathematical research.

An attendant problem was the growing separation of the disciplines. In reviewing Mrs. Somerville's 1834 book, *On the Connection of the Physical Sciences,* Whewell approvingly stressed the word *connection* and spoke with concern about the "dismemberment of the sciences." The "disintegration goes on," he wrote, "like that of a great empire falling to pieces." It was not simply that the mathematician was turning away from the chemist, the chemist from the naturalist; there was also estrangement within the disciplines. "The mathematician, left to himself, divides himself into a pure mathematician and a mixed mathematician, who soon part company."[18] By the middle of the century, Henry Acland, no longer riding out with Lord and Lady Lovelace, was spurring his colleagues to establish a natural history museum at Oxford to bring together the various scientific disciplines. There was need to unite the sciences; ironically, there was also need to accelerate specialization. What Whewell feared in 1834 was indeed beginning to happen in mathematics with the growth of symbolical algebra and non-Euclidean geometry—the loss of certainty about what mathematics was and about the kind of philosophical foundation it rested upon. At the start of the fourth decade of the nineteenth century, however, the overriding concern was not yet debate between science and scripture but agitation for organization and for government support.

If British science in the early nineteenth century was still a pastime for intellectuals, as Babbage suggested, then mathematics could be pursued only by those whose leisure was undisturbed by other claims.[19] There was need, therefore, for government subsidy and for an official supportive community of practicing scientists. The founding of the Astronomical Society (Babbage was first secretary from 1820 to 1824) was an important step in establishing scientific fraternity. But larger actions were needed. One was the opening in 1827 of University College, London, called by the historian E. J. Hobsbawm an "alternative to the somnolence of Oxford and Cambridge."[20] That year, Augustus De Morgan became its first professor of mathematics and found a congenial atmosphere, relatively tolerant of political and religious dissenters and receptive to technology. But a more significant event was to follow in September 1831, when the British Association for the Advancement of Science was founded, called by Hobsbawm an alternative to the "aristocratic torpor of the degenerate Royal Society." Founding statements of the BAAS reflected the Analyticals' call for a working-scientist admissions policy and for support of mathematical research as part of a "developing spirit of social improvement."[21] Of course, between idealism and reality there fell a shadow. The association got carried away at times with self-congratulation (and was called then the "British Ass"); it also tolerated cranks, to the parodic amusement of Ada and Babbage's friend Charles Dickens, who lampooned it in 1838, in *Bentley's Miscellany*, as the "Mudfog Association for the Advancement of Everything." Dedicated to internationalism, the association could be childishly parochial; seeking to connect disciplines, it often ranked them politically, with pure mathematics still dominating. Babbage was a trustee of the association for five years; not surprising, high on the list of possible projects for association approval and government subsidy was the Analytical Engine. But Babbage did not always help his own cause. He did not attend the society's opening meeting at York, though David Brewster begged him "on . . . [his] knees" to be there. Babbage was too busy in London arguing about his engines. Yet it was at the 1833 association meeting that Babbage met the Belgian astronomer and statistician Quetelet (1796–1874), who would be instrumental in promoting plans for the Analytical Engine, and it was at the 1834 meeting that Babbage helped form the first statistics society.

A passion was growing among Cambridge intellectuals for facts of all kinds, to be used not just for navigation but for political economy and meteorology, and perhaps even by Panizzi for the new cataloguing of the British Museum Library.[22] Visiting various mechanical institutes and workrooms with her mother, on Babbage's recommendations, Ada would have been aware of mathematical considerations like these not usually addressed by the universities. Although internal politics and conflicting scientific needs were often apparent at British Association meetings, the very existence of this organization, the first official challenge to the hegemony of the Royal Society, was important in eventually bringing about changes of the kind Babbage had been advocating. If engineers and mechanists were not yet at home in the association, at least debate about priorities was out in the open. The movement for reform had begun, though it would not become official at Cambridge until mid-century. By then, however, only the scientifically knowledgeable would have noticed and appreciated the change. In 1856, four years after Ada's death, Lady Byron wrote a beseeching letter to an aging Augustus De Morgan. Would he please tutor Ada's son Ralph: "In *my* opinion it would be worth a year of Cambridge with *all* its studies," she implored.[23] It was a remark she would most likely have made twenty-five years earlier, for many different reasons—intellectual, social, personal—but the fact remains that in Ada's day, if not still in Ralph's, private tutoring still surpassed formal schooling, particularly in mathematics and especially so for young ladies. Education for them at a pre-university level would certainly not have satisfied anyone with intellectual curiosity. Rather than suffer greatly by not attending Cambridge, young women of Ada Byron's talents—and young men whose mathematical interests were not mainstream—could and would do far better on their own.

[CHAPTER 3]

The Programming
of Ada Lovelace

Although Lady Byron expected the tutor Dr. William King to
succeed in his moral "operation" on thirteen-year-old
Ada's brain—instilling discipline by means of mathematics—
discipline would be about all he would instill. A kind man, King
was not particularly interested in mathematics. His last two
works were on scrofula, in 1851 (he had a medical degree), and
"Thoughts on the Teaching of Christ," published posthumously
in 1872. He had been twelfth "wrangler" at Cambridge (a
debater on the tripos) and, as he admitted to Ada, this rank did
not include "men of the first class." His primary interests, like
Lady Byron's, were philanthropic—to bring morality and manners to the poor. Now they would include as well the education
of a virtuous Ada Byron. Ada's letters to and from King,
especially those in 1834, when she was "not entirely a beginner"
in Euclid, arithmetic, and algebra, disclose a somewhat knowledgeable eighteen-year-old asking thoughtful questions about
geometry, and a well-meaning but traditional pedagogue unable
to keep up. In the spring of 1834 Ada was reading Dionysius
Lardner's *Euclid*, the one she believed "most approved by mathematicians," but her interest may have been less in Euclid than
in Lardner, who was lecturing at the Mechanics' Institute on
Babbage's Difference Engine.

"You will soon puzzle me in your studies," King wrote Ada
that same spring, and he referred to his own training as conventional: "We *got up* a set of books and seldom went out of

them. . . ." Ada liked freer scope: "I do not consider that I know a proposition until I can imagine to myself a figure in the air, and go through the construction & demonstration without any book or assistance whatever. . . ." Should she keep to pure mathematics for a while, before going on to the sciences? she queried. She was asking the wrong person. She was also restless, she wrote King; her imagination was "running wild," and "very *close & intense* application to subjects of a scientific nature" would keep her occupied." Her words sound guarded. Was she aware that her letters to King would be given over to Lady Byron, who had already established such practice with several confidants? In any case, to Ada's invitation for restraints against a loosening fancy, King accommodated by recommending "a complete Cambridge course"[1] and the usual textbooks, though one text, Vince's *Plane and Spherical Trigonometry*, had been the particular complaint of more than one Cambridge undergraduate, including Frederick Pollock, the senior wrangler in 1806 who, years later, in response to a request to assess his Cambridge studies, wrote that Vince was a "bungler" and "utterly insensible of mathematical beauty."[2] Regardless, King was a good choice for domesticating Ada's rampant imagination. Mathematics, he wrote his young charge, because they require "*undivided* attention" and because they "have no connection with the *feelings* of life," cannot possibly lead to any objectionable thoughts.

Despite his standing with Lady Byron, King was not the only surgeon she engaged to instill virtue. Chief among those who were also asked to guide Ada into moral and mathematical maturity was William Frend, whose daughter, Sophia, would marry Augustus De Morgan. Frend (1757–1841), who had been expelled from university residence in 1793 for rebellious pamphleteering, was an old man when Lady Byron asked him to instruct Ada. Years later, in 1841, commenting to Sophia on Frend's death, Ada spoke kindly of her mentor, though his "age and infirmities," she noted, had kept their exchanges infrequent. Ada was respectfully polite. Lady Byron had been a favorite pupil of William Frend and remained a lifelong correspondent, but their letters, numerous and on various topics, do not include significant discussion of mathematics. Although Frend had been second wrangler at Cambridge, most of his publications were not on technical subjects, and his tutelage of Ada in the mathematical sciences can be assumed to have been competent but uninspired. His biographer, respectful and admiring, concedes his sometimes "priggish" and "preaching attitude."

A note from Ada to Sophia on February 11, 1829, thanks her and Frend for sending on some "excellent descriptions" in astronomy, then gives what sounds like a progress report. The sense is of an accounting to be made to the proper authorities, which was probably true. For all his political radicalism, however, William Frend was conservative to the point of being old-fashioned both in morals and, to judge by the movement for a new algebra that Peacock had helped start some years earlier, in mathematics. Indeed, the *Dictionary of National Biography* refers to Frend as a "noted oppugner of all that distinguishes Algebra from Arithmetic"—a position that would have set him against concepts about number inherent in Babbage's plans for his Analytical Engine. An old-fashioned rationalist, Frend rejected negative and imaginary magnitudes, afraid they would bolster superstition by allowing the mysterious to intrude upon God's most reasonable discipline. Like others who rejected such "numbers," Freud was disturbed by paradoxical definitions that made "less than nothing" a quantity, and by numerical concepts that had no place in the world of everyday measurement or calculation. The traditional position was that "numbers" had to have meaning in the sense of real world or geometric correspondences. The symbolical algebraists, however, posited number as a symbol in a logical system designed by mathematicians, not God. Such a position violated the view of mathematics as absolute certainty and threatened the Platonic association of mathematics and divinity that had ruled Cambridge for centuries and that Frend had defended in his *Principles of Algebra* (1796). Later on, Frend wrote a play, possibly with Sophia, mocking such "numbers" and parodying the new algebraists for their willingness to rely on undefined signs and symbols governed by man-made laws. The protagonist of the play was his son-in-law, Augustus De Morgan, Ada's tutor in 1841.[4] Ada, of course, working with Babbage and De Morgan, both active in the development of symbolic algebra, did not subscribe to

Frend's views. As she was composing the "Notes," Ada wrote to Babbage for "something more" about how to manage such numbers, and while it is not certain how Babbage may have answered, "Note A" pays homage to the Analytical Engine's potential to deal with them: "We cannot forbear suggesting one practical result which it appears to us must be greatly facilitated by the independent manner in which the [analytical] engine orders and combines its *operations:* we allude to the attainment of those combinations into which *imaginary quantities* enter."[5]

Frend, Lady Byron's ally, was expected to keep Lady Byron informed about Ada's work and attitude, a function Sophia may also have assumed. As might be expected, the virtuous Frend had taken Lady Byron's side in 1816 during the separation. In 1815, he had referred to Byron as the author of the lyrical *Hebrew Melodies* (1815)—as if the first two cantos of the thinly disguised autobiographical *Childe Harold* (1812) had never been written. (The third canto, Byron's favorite, beginning and ending with an apostrophe to Ada, was not published until 1816.) Lady Byron consulted William Frend extensively on educational matters, but she consulted a great many people, as the formidable Byron/Lovelace manuscript collection attests. Fortunately for Ada, another of Lady Byron's choices was more knowledgeable about mathematics.

Mary Fairfax Somerville (1780–1872), a remarkable figure in Victorian science, was more productive as the wife of Dr. Somerville than as young Mary Fairfax or as Mrs. Samuel Greig. As Mary Fairfax, a young upper-class Scotswoman and daughter of a vice-admiral, she had encountered opposition to her studying mathematics. Later on, as Mrs. Greig, the wife of an unsympathetic Russian naval captain, she met less resistance but gained no support. As Mrs. William Somerville, however, the wife of a medical doctor and cousin (she had been widowed three years after marrying Greig), she moved into the intellectual sphere, becoming a grand dame of science. Her translation of Laplace's *Celestial Mechanics* (1831), the great success of *On the Connection of the Physical Sciences* (1834), which she wrote under her own name, and her precedent-setting election (with Caroline Herschel) to the Royal Astronomical Society were just a few of the reasons why the *Morning Post* referred to her when she died as the queen of nineteenth-century science. She knew all the leading scientists of the day and kept up with events on the Continent. "The latest experiments and speculations in every part of Europe are referred to," wrote William Whewell admiringly in his review of *On the Connection of the Physical Sciences.* Ada Byron was her intellectual beneficiary. In 1834 Ada was still writing to Dr. King about arithmetic and algebra, attending scientific lectures with his wife, and submitting queries on science to William Frend, but Mrs. Somerville, whom Ada finally met that year, was to become her favorite chaperone. Mrs. Somerville sent Ada mathematics books, advised her on study, set problems for her, and, above all, talked to her young protegée about mathematics.[6] Some of that conversation was about Babbage and his engines. Babbage and Mrs. Somerville had been friends for years and corresponded regularly.

Mrs. Somerville's expertise and reputation were such that Sophia (Mrs. De Morgan by 1837) suggests in her memoirs, *Threescore Years and Ten,* that Mrs. Somerville was a kind of touchstone for mathematically gifted women. The occasion was a recollection of an obscure but talented female mathematician whom Sophia and her father had met at the home of the learned and gregarious Baron Francis Maseres (1731–1824), an occasional mathematician, historian, and reformer. In Sophia's account, the obscure lady is said to be second only to Mrs. Somerville.

> Baron Maseres was really generous and liberal in his estimate of women's learning, though he certainly must have thought their powers very far below those of men. I heard him express admiration for a lady who had learnt Greek and Latin—to some extent an unusual acquirement then—. . . . My father introduced him to a Miss Lousada, a Jewish lady of great intellectual power. She was a mathematician, and had translated Diophantus, and edited or annotated Mascheroni [interesting for his constructions, without ruler, of Euclid]. She had written many volumes of university history, and would have been at any time a very distinguished scholar, not far second to Mrs. Somerville. She had, I imagine, few opportunities of meeting persons who could exchange ideas with her on scientific subjects and her much anticipated interview with Maseres amazed my father and mother. The two mathematicians

plunged at once into deep water. The entrance of my mother being so little noticed that she left them to settle some disputed question, and returned after half an hour to find them just where they were.[7]

Maseres, incidentally, is one of the "fantastic forms" Charles Lamb invokes in "Essay on the Old Benchers of the Inner Temple"—"Baron Maseres, who walks (or did till very lately) in the costume of the reign of George the Second." A "character" with a well-known London salon, Maseres was regarded as a mathematician of limited accomplishments and suspect views. Although Priestly wrote that Maseres's mathematics was "original and excellent," the DNB records (somewhat extravagantly) that, like William Frend, Maseres set himself "against the world" by maintaining an opposition to negative numbers and to distinctions between algebra and arithmetic. One of their pet projects, however, might have interested Babbage and Ada had they all lived closer in time: to calculate "more decimal places than any one would want and to reprint the works of all who had done the same thing." Despite his mathematical eccentricity, Maseres's contribution to the history of mathematics, though indirect, was important. In presiding over a salon that attracted leading intellectuals, Maseres, and Babbage later on, gave women what they could not have had in clubs, in scientific associations, or at universities—the opportunity to associate with leading scientific and literary intellectuals. Of course, upper-class women could do so in their own great houses, but they would be expected to assume hostess roles, a constant and time-consuming activity. In the salons of others, women intellectuals were free of such social obligations.

But in another sense the salon might press intellectual women. As Miss Lousada was held "not far second" to Mrs. Somerville in intellectual powers, just so other women intellectuals were often held second to Mrs. Somerville in decorum. Self-effacing and gracious, Mrs. Somerville was extremely popular on the London scene with both men and women. That she did not become famous until well into her fifties, an unusually late mathematical coming-of-age, suggests that admirers did not note the personal cost of such delayed achievement. An ostensible model for aspiring young female mathematicians like Ada Byron, Mrs. Somerville nonetheless held views typical of her time and conducted herself in society in ways that always occasioned admirable comment. When she left for Italy for reasons of health and study, Harriet Martineau noted the loss to society. How unfortunate that Mrs. Somerville should spend the last third of her life in a country so unworthy of her.[8] Although Mrs. Somerville achieved international recognition for her work in science, the impression she gave first was of an intelligent women, wife, and mother, who seemed to "know her place."

With Mrs. Somerville and her daughters, Ada Byron made scientific visits—heard lectures, attended scientific demonstrations, saw new devices and inventions—though the daughters were not much interested. They also went to hear music, Ada's passion: "I am going this evening to my friend Mrs. Somerville's to stay the night," she wrote her future husband, a month before they were married. "She has kindly offered to take me to a Concert, which my love of music could not resist."[9] There were preparations for the wedding to attend to, of course, but there was also mathematics. Binomial expansions could count for more than ballgowns.

London was in high scientific and mechanical gear in the 1830s, and for Ada it was a heady time, suggesting a "bride of science" in the making as much as William King's bride. Ada, not yet Lady King, needed a chaperone to visit Babbage's studio. Caught up by excitement and in "great anxiety" about Babbage's machine, Ada wrote to Mrs. Somerville that sometimes her "eagerness" about the engines caused her to overlook notes to be answered; please forgive her. Mrs. Somerville, affable, helpful, proper, calm, may have been a cautionary influence on the headstrong but somewhat aloof Ada Byron. Mrs. Somerville was a woman with reputation in mathematical sciences at a time when most women with interests in natural philosophy took up geology or botany, disciplines that did not depend upon mathematical notation or formulas. And most women were content to be popularizers or teachers. Certainly no member of the aristocracy, man or woman, would want to admit to practicing a profession—a life associated with money or trade. With great panache, Byron had once declared that he was not a poet but a gentleman, that his function as lord was not to do but merely to be. But then gentlemen had access to the world of ideas much more easily than women. Women such as Mrs. Somerville and Ada Lovelace were not dissuaded from following mathematical paths as long as they stayed within bounds—restrictions of class as much as of gender.

There were indeed women in mid-century England who signed their names to mathematical articles in popular journals, and there were influential periodicals, such as the *Edinburgh Review*, that lent intellectual women psychological support. As the historians of science Morrell and Thackray show, "It was still possible in the early Victorian world for the enthusiastic devotee who lacked formal training to make major contributions to the scientific enterprise at the research level"; and many of these amateurs were women.[10] Although the *Ladies' Diary* (or *Woman's Almanac*, 1704–1841), the most popular of the mathematical periodicals, encouraged women to join wit with beauty, it attracted serious amateurs of both sexes.[11] Not a prestigious publication like *Taylor's Scientific Memoirs*, where Ada's translations and "Notes" appeared, the *Ladies' Diary* was nonetheless a respectable place to pose mathematical problems and sustain debate. The *Edinburgh Review* notes that along with the *Diary's* more fanciful material, some of it downright silly, "much good mathematics" was buried in its pages.[12] In fact, since there were few science periodicals in England until the 1830s, technical articles often appeared in general periodicals like the *Ladies' Diary*. It may have been something similar that originally sparked Mrs. Somerville's interest in mathematics. At a tea party one afternoon, she recalled years later, young Mary Fairfax had been given a ladies' fashion magazine that contained a puzzle, the answer to which was given in strange symbols. These symbols turned out to be algebra. And that magazine became her introduction to the world of Euclidean geometry and number.

A successful woman in the world of mathematical science, albeit not an original investigator, Mrs. Somerville did not consider herself bound to vindicate the rights of women. Nor did Ada. There was no need. Mrs. Somerville could not be admitted to the Royal Society, even though a bust of her stood in the hall in tribute, but she enjoyed a reputation for excellence that brought her praise from men—though, admittedly, some of that admiration must have been given for her deferential attitude. The year before the British Association would hold its Oxford meeting, William Buckland wondered what to do about Mrs. Somerville, the most significant English woman in science, How could she be ignored? Then again, how could she be invited to the all-male convocation at conservative Oxford? Some members of the association complained that ladies had ruined the tone of lectures at the Royal Institution and that women were elbowing their way into general sessions of the association, squeezing into restricted seminars and displacing men. Science, the "serious philosophical union of working men," was inconsistent with female noise and numbers.[13] What to do about Mrs. Somerville? Fortunately, the sensitive lady sent word—through her husband, naturally—that she would not attend. And President-Elect William Buckland judged her response correctly: Mrs. Somerville, he announced, chose not to come because she thought that women in general ought not attend association meetings. William Whewell blessed her common sense and female nature to accommodate. In women, he said, the heart tended to rule the head. Still, Whewell acknowledged the profundity and clarity of women philosophers in general and of Mrs. Somerville in particular.[14]

Intellectual life in mid-nineteenth-century England was conducted largely in private clubs, at universities (closed to women until Cambridge reluctantly opened its doors in 1890), and in other upper-class male bastions. Scientific associations, with the exception of the botanical and the horticultural societies of London, did not permit female members, but exclusion was not as pervasive as some critics have claimed. Class and power could go a long way to remedy deficiencies. The increasing presence of women in lectures and exhibitions suggests that discrimination against women was felt only if they demanded leadership roles. Although none of the 353 members who signed the meeting book of the first British Association at York in 1831 were women, they were in attendance. Kept out of the special discussion groups where advanced scientific debates were held, they were allowed in to the general session in the evening. It was a period of slow change, but of change, nonetheless. When King's College was opened in 1832 as part of the University of London and women petitioned to hear Charles Lyell lecture on geology, Babbage and others, insistent on having women admitted, briefly prevailed. Later on that year, the traditionalists regained the ground, but not before Mrs. Somerville, with her daughters and Ada, had attended lectures there.

Spending time with Mrs. Somerville, whose fame had begun with translations, the young Ada Byron must have seen how advantageous it was to know languages. The growing movement in the 1830s to internationalize science required expertise in French and German, not generally a credential of the educated. In 1831, according to one Professor Moll, a scholar from Utrecht, whose 1831 "On the Alleged Decline of Science" was a response to Babbage, "the number of those who acquire a smattering of French is very small, and still smaller is the number of those who know enough German."[15] Facility in French, a language Ada had been studying since childhood, no doubt influenced her decision in 1842 to translate Menabrea's article for *Taylor's Scientific Memoirs*, and some knowledge of German allowed her to consider doing translations for Taylor from that language.[16] The fact that her Menabrea translation appeared anonymously, however, was no slight to women. Since translations were not usually signed, a case might even be made that Ada received favored treatment from Richard Taylor because each of the "Notes" was initiated.

Thus, although women had a more difficult time than men if they wanted to study mathematics, they were making their presence felt, even if some reasons for tolerating them were cynical. Babbage, a constant advocate of the bonnet brigade, shrewdly argued that if bluestockings were given (blue) tickets to British Association meetings, more men would attend, and if more men attended, there would be more money for the central purse. By increasing the number of upper-class people interested in science, Babbage foresaw a closer association among the academic community, wealthy families, and manufacturers. Why, one of the landed gentry might even be interested in financing a calculating engine! At least in this calculation, Babbage was eminently practical. But though the presence of women at association meetings was good politics, Babbage was also sympathetic. Was it merely editing style that caused him to write to Ada on September 9, 1843, as his "dear and much admired Interpreter" and then, three days later, to call her his "fair Interpret*ress*"?[17] Might Babbage have been a bit uneasy about upstaging his hard-working "fairy," as Ada sometimes called herself? Ada and Babbage had had sharp words the previous month over his suggestion to delay publication of the "Notes." And now, one month later, with the "Notes" barely published, Babbage had gone into print again (in the *Philosophical Magazine*) with another version of his quarrel with the government—without once mentioning his hard-working assistant and expositor. But if "dear old Bab" really understood his willful protegée, which is highly probable, he would have known that she wanted to announce herself to the world.

Though socially diffident and guided by expectations of propriety, Ada could be direct, bold, and emphatic. It is difficult to imagine her subscribing to the kind of intellectual humility expressed by Mrs. Somerville in her *Autobiography:*

> In the climax of my great success the approbation of some of the first scientific men of the age and of the public in general I was highly gratified, but much less elated than might have been expected, for although I had recorded in a clear point of view some of the most refined and difficult analytical processes and astronomical discoveries, I was conscious that I had never made a discovery myself, that I had no originality. I have perseverance and intelligence but no genius [talent], that spark from heaven is not granted to the sex, we are of the earth . . . whether higher powers may be allotted to us in another existence God knows, original genius in science at least is hopeful in this.[18]

Ada undoubtedly heard such sentiments, expressions of the time. "Original genius" was not resident in women: women were not constitutionally fit for hard intellectual work. Mrs. Somerville, a complex and compassionate woman, endorsed these attitudes, but in her later years, long after Ada had died, she was eager to say something else. In 1869, two years before her death, too old, she declared to compose a formal essay, she wrote a letter in which she lamented the "low estimation" in which "our intellect has hitherto been held. It was a "prejudice," she said, that high intelligence would ruin women as wives and mothers. A woman who would neglect her family for study would neglect her family for any reason. As for the argument that the constitution of girls weakened them for serious pursuits—the very theme she had sounded for years— she wrote now that it was "by no means the case," if studies were "taken progressively." She noted approvingly that the University of London was now granting diplomas to governesses and that "the members of the illustrious University of Cambridge" were generously espousing "our cause."[19] But her assessment was not quite accurate. Just four years earlier, in 1865, *Household Chess Magazine* suggested that women entering the correspondence tournament do so by using "the name of some male relative (a father or a brother), unless her opponent is a lady also." As for face-to-face chess tournaments for women, adversaries of the idea were still claiming in 1897 that such a tournament would be a farce and that women "would collapse with nervous strain at having to play two rounds a day for 10 days."[20]

Florence Nightingale would have agreed with the observation but might have offered sympathetic arguments about probable cause. Her passionate statements on behalf of ambitious women illustrate the degree to which talented and frustrated women sometimes felt driven. The degree was far beyond what either Ada Lovelace or Mrs. Somerville would ever have contemplated writing. Like Ada, Florence Nightingale was well-born and intellectually ambitious. She was also manifestly bored with her family and social life, sounding at times suicidal. In 1852, the year Ada died, Florence Nightingale started on an autobiographical account of her discontents. Called *Cassandra,* it decried "claims of the social life" that prevented women from spending time on study. And nowhere, she wrote, was this unfairness and frustration more in evidence than in mathematics—the pursuit least compatible with the demands made upon women by society. Despite opposition from family and society, Florence Nightingale persevered. Her case, however, could hardly be said to be representative.

The belief that women intellectuals were subject to physical and mental injury was held not only by Mrs. Somerville for most of her life but, more significantly, by Augustus De Morgan, who worried about Ada's health in the same breath that he praised her intelligence. De Morgan, a key figure in mathematics because of his prolific writings on the differential and integral calculus, history of mathematics, indexing, geometry, and mathematical logic, became another of Ada's tutors in 1840, a particularly stellar acquisition. A Fellow of the Astronomical Society and of the Society for the Diffusion of Useful Knowledge, and cofounder of the London Mathematical Society, De Morgon was known to be fastitious about detail. If Ada Lovelace sent him reams of equations, exercises, and proofs, it may not have been because her grasp of elementary subjects was tenuous,[21] but because, as her numerous mathematical letters to De Morgan show, she was anxious and meticulous and eager to please. In any case, while also eager to please, De Morgan did not descend to slippery praise with Lady Byron, and the presence of his wife, no great admirer of Ada Lovelace, might have served as a corrective. Thus in 1844, when De Morgon wrote to Lady Byron that had any young beginner been about to go to Cambridge with powers equal to Ada's, that person would have made "an original mathematical investigator, perhaps of first rate eminence," there is no reason to think he was insincere.

That same letter, however, also shows that De Morgan accepted the prejudices of his day against women in science, but he proffered his belief that Ada's intellect was superior even to Mrs. Somerville's. He wrote that he had never expressed his opinion of Ada directly to her, but that he was indeed impressed by her "original" mathematical mind.

> . . . I feel bound to tell you that the power of thinking . . . which Lady L. has always shown from the beginning of my correspondence with her, has been something so utterly out of the common way for any beginner, man or woman, that this power must be duly considered by her friends, with reference to the question whether they should urge or check her obvious determination to try not only to reach but to get beyond, the present bounds of knowledge.[22]

It was not simply her degree of intellectual power, De Morgan noted, but its quality. With a dig at the Cambridge system, which turned on competitive mathematics examinations and traditional curricula, De Morgan declared that Ada's aptitude at grasping the "strong points and the real difficulties of first *principles*" would have lowered her chances of being a wrangler at Cambridge. Although De Morgan revered Mrs. Somerville, Ada seemed to him to have the more impressive mind. Mrs. Somerville never moved beyond the "*details* of mathematical *work*," and thus she was able to enjoy society, attend to ordinary cares, be a successful scholar, wife, and mother. Ada, he predicted, would "take quite a different route." It was not simply that De Morgan regarded Mrs. Somerville as a good mathematical practitioner while suggesting that Ada was a creative thinker; he was also implying that Mrs. Somerville was limited, perhaps, also in her grasp of details. He cited her "ignorance of the nature of force" by pointing out that she had given it as dv / dt (the formula for acceleration; the formula for force is ma, where m = mass and a = acceleration). Mrs. Somerville had confused momentum and velocity. "Lady L" would never have allowed such an oversight, he wrote, and it "made him smile" to imagine her reading such a mistake, much less writing it.[23]

Along with his high praise, however, De Morgan also expressed his sense that intense study would aggravate the risk to Ada's health. All women mathematicians have knowledge and power, he wrote, but only Maria Agnesi (1718–1799) had truly wrestled with intellectual difficulties and shown a man's strength in overcoming them. In an earlier note to Lady Byron, De Morgan had expressed concern about Ada which, surprisingly, was dismissed by Lady Byron. Writing for herself and for Lord Lovelace, Lady Byron asserted that if Ada would "but attend to her stomach, her brain would be capable even of more than she has ever imposed on it—."[24] People may report what they want, Lady Byron had written to De Morgan, but she herself had made careful observations and concluded (consistent with her observations of Ada in childhood) that "The consciousness of making progress in science seems . . . an essential element in her happiness." The more she worked at mathematics, the happier she was. Lady Byron would indeed be vindicated.

But De Morgan persisted in his views, arguing in a way that would suggest even greater admiration for Ada's talents. As much as he had liked the "Notes," he wrote Lady Byron, he felt that they were not the best of what Ada could do. They merely suggested what might be accomplished "when the subject had not entirely engrossed her attention . . ."; imagine what might follow if Lady Lovelace could sustain the "struggle between the mind and body" that total intellectual commitment would demand. "That tract about Babbage's machine is a pretty thing enough," he continued, but he could, he thought, "produce a series of extracts, out of Lady Lovelace's first queries upon new subjects, which would make a mathematician see that it was no criterion of what might be expected from her."

Frend, Somerville, De Morgan, others—mathematicians and scientists—these were valuable guides for the aspiring young student. What they would not have given her—indeed, what should come from within but often requires the stimulus of a particular person—was direction. For this, Ada wrote Babbage late in 1839, after the birth of her third child, she required a certain kind of *"Man,"* a "peculiar man," one who could address her "peculiar *way* of learning," call forth her sense of having "the *power* of going just as far as I like in such [mathematical] pursuits," and answer the "very decided" taste, nay *"passion* I have for them. . . ."[25] That taste was such, she added Byroni-cally, that it *"must* be gratified."

Ada Lovelace had met the socially active mathematician and inventor Charles Babbage at a party on June 5, 1833, and had been instantly taken with his brilliance and charm. She was eighteen and had recently been presented at court. Being at Babbage's studio, however, would prove more exciting. History offers a few such men, geniuses obsessed with matters of the mind for whom the worldly life is also important, and Babbage was preeminently one of them. Despite the death of his beloved wife, of two children, and of his father in 1827, and notwith-standing poor health and constant exasperation with workmen, Charles Babbage could be extraordinarily good company: witty, clever, charming. Harriet Martineau included him in her discus-sion of eminent and vain men, but she added that he was "greatly misunderstood" and praised his fun, good humor and "domestic tenderness," all of which put him in great demand in drawing rooms and made 1 Dorset Street a place to be. "Doing the Babbage," it was said, was a stellar event in any season.

Two weeks after meeting Babbage, Lady Byron and Ada visited him at his London studio, where the Difference Engine was on display, along with the Silver Lady. Small-scale machinery then was considered part of salon decor, crafted as much for aesthetic delight as for practical application. Pascal's arithmetic machine (1647) and Leibniz's calculator (1674), for example, sophisticated calculating instruments, were also beautiful fabrications.[26] Babbage's machine, a handsome affair of gears, columns, wheels, and disks, delighted visitors. Its popularity might be gauged by the ease with which Harriet Martineau used it in 1834 in a humorous reference to a certain well-known poet: "Taking the facts of his life together with his utterances, I believe the philosophy and moralizing of Coleridge to be much like the action of Babbage's machine; and his utterance to be about equal in wonder to the numerical results given out by the mechanician's instrument."[27]

In her June 1833 letter to Dr. William King, the same to whom she had entrusted Ada's head for moral guidance, Lady Byron commented briefly on the "*thinking* machine" she and Ada had just seen at Babbage's. "It raised several Nos. to the 2nd & 3rd powers, and extracted the root of a Quadratic Equation," she reported, but despite her own mathematical training, she had but "faint glimpses of the [mathematical] principles by which it worked."[28] In an earlier note to King, she had referred to Babbage's regard for his machine as being like a child's for his "plaything." Lady Byron admired Babbage but seemed to be comfortable with him only when he was talking mathematics, and especially when he connected mathematics to larger, philosophical concerns. Then there could be "sublimity" in his views. Otherwise, she concluded, Babbage was "*finical* about his furniture, and occupied with other trifles."

Evenings at Babbage's during the mid-1830s could be hectic, with the company sometimes numbering two hundred a night. The Silver Lady, nude when Babbage got her in 1834, was clothed one year later by Babbage and his friends and became the source of more amusement. Babbage joked about her with

Ada, one month before her marriage, and sent her cards for his last two parties of the season, noting playfully that the Silver Lady would appear "in new dresses and decorations," and with a turban, which he had just pinned up. The reception so far, he conceded, had been lukewarm, but "I suppose perseverance will do much for decorating the out as well as the inside of heads"; he trusted he would do better as a decorator next year.[29] He would, but as interior decorator: Ada was about to place herself in his service and to insist on staying there. It is doubtful that Babbage would have written Ada about his Silver Lady had she been as serious about life as her redoubtable mother. Lady Byron preferred to credit Dr. King for Ada's intellectual development. His "conversing & reading" with his young charge on philosophical subjects had obviously enabled Ada to move with ease among the scientific people she had been meeting recently.

Contrary to Lady Byron's "faint glimpses" of the Difference Engine's principles, Ada's response, as recorded by Sophia Frend, was a cool, knowing understanding.

> While other visitors gazed at the working of this beautiful instrument with the sort of expression, and I dare say the sort of feeling, that some savages are said to have shown on first seeing a looking-glass or hearing a gun—if, indeed, they had as strong an idea of its marvellousness—Miss Byron, young as she was, understood its working, and saw the great beauty of the invention. She had read the Differential Calculus to some extent. . . .[30]

Although Sophia gets her engines confused, referring to an "analytical" engine, which never existed, the "slip" may suggest that there were discussions about the Analytical Engine between Augustus De Morgan and Ada, a likelihood, considering their concentrated correspondence in the years directly preceding composition of the "Notes." The word *analytical* was identified with Continental mathematics and with the calculus that Ada had been studying. Sophia, not always reliable and not disposed to praise the "vain" and "egotistical" daughter of her friend Lady Byron, probably gives a generally truthful account. Admittedly no judge of mathematical ability, she confessed that when she went with her father to Baron Maseres, where she had seen Miss Lousada, she heard "a good deal of mathematics which . . . [she] did not understand." Nonetheless, Sophia was the daughter of William Frend and, by 1837, the wife of one of Britain's best-known mathematicians. Although her memoirs did not appear until 1889, she may have earlier discussed Ada's "great mathematical power" with Augustus De Morgan, who died in 1871. That Ada was deserving of high praise had certainly been De Morgan's own assessment.

For Babbage, there was undoubtedly special pleasure in finding a socially prominent and intellectual, albeit young, admirer. In 1834, the year Ada first saw plans for the analytical machine, Babbage had just determined that the Difference Engine should be left as it was and that a new engine should absorb his concentrations. His thoughts had been prompted in part by experiments in getting the Difference Engine to do "carries" in addition, fast and simply, an extremely complex process.[31] By the summer of 1834, shortly before Ada and Mrs. Somerville would visit, Babbage concluded that it would be better to start on a new design rather than try to modify the earlier one again. Critical to his new idea was what he called "foreseeing." He envisioned a machine that could "anticipate" moves and react accordingly, even reverse itself and alter operations. He believed that such a machine could change the destiny of science.

The year 1834 was also a crucial one for Ada. In her nineteenth year, she was near marriage to the eligible but rather staid William King, a Cambridge friend of Woronzow Greig, an arrangement that would only increase the influence of her dominating mother. For Ada, Babbage's combination of genius and social ease must have been extremely attractive. Her own life, until recently, had been a series of mysterious and undiagnosed physical disorders. Socially and medically constricted, having been alone a good deal (Lady Byron had often been away on litigious or philanthropic business), Ada had been pursuing mathematics in a way that suggests obligation more than pleasure. Her mathematical correspondents were usually tutors and friends, older than she, chosen by her mother, or clearly not her intellectual equals. One friend, for example, a godchild of Lady Byron, Annabella Acheson (Lady Gosford's daughter), had been having trouble with geometry. Their "Sentimental Mathematical Correspondence between two Young Ladies of Rank"

(Ada's suggested title) takes on a forced affectionate tone.[32] The more Ada strove to make Euclidean points perfectly clear, with reams of proofs and definitions, the more she seemed aware of her own maturity and apologized for it at the same time that she proffered friendship. In Babbage she found humor, indepen- dence, and, above all, originality.

The Difference Engine, as Ada saw, was an ingenious applica- tion of an old school exercise, the method of finite differences. Actually, the use of the method for calculating machines was not new, though Babbage understandably thought so. Like his contemporary William Blake, and like many other knowledge- able English men of science, Charles Babbage was more inspired than influenced. Though the Royal Society in 1823 had referred to Difference Engine No. 1, a working model, as a "machine for calculation" (Babbage used the terms *machine* and *engine* inter- changeably) the name "Difference Engine," for the version Babbage had assembled by 1833, was appropriate, reflecting its mathematical principle. The method of differences involves a successive computation of "differences" until a stage yields constant differences, meaning that the next difference would result in all zeroes; at this point, the process is complete. The number of times necessary to go through this process until constant differences are arrived at is determined by the degree of the polynomial (an algebraic expression, such as $ax^2 + bx + c$, consisting of sums of constants, multiplied by a variable raised to a power), which is to be computed by the engine. When the function is not a polynomial, the engine would work with polynomial approximations.[33] Later on, in thinking about the Analytical Engine, Babbage would consider a machine that could calculate without needing a fixed order of differences.

Babbage himself gave an example of how the method of differences would work, but, as historians have pointed out, his explanations are not that easy to follow. The squares of the first natural numbers—1, 2, 3, 4, 5, and so on—are 1, 4, 9, 16, 25; and the first differences between the squares are, respectively, 3, 5, 7, 9. If the differences between these first differences are then taken, thereby obtaining second differences, the results would be 2, 2, 2—constants—and the differences between these, in turn, would be zero. By knowing the constant difference and some starting numbers in the method, one can "go back," adding differences, thereby obtaining further values in the original sequence. Thus a table of values can be generated. In Babbage's example, since the constant difference is 2, the number after 9 in the sequence of first differences is 11, and hence the square after 25 is 36 (11 added to the last square).

The idea is that if one has to compute many values for tables, it is easier to do it by adding differences; the addition is done by working backwards from the constant differences. Additions eliminate the need for multiplication. As Williams and others point out, a difference engine is "simply a machine which is capable of both storing a series of numbers and performing additions with those numbers." What Babbage perceived was that this process "supplied a general principle by which all tables generated by polynomials might be computed through limited intervals, by one uniform process" (*Passages*, Chapter 5). First, the law of a given arithmetic series would be set by hand, and then toothed wheels, gears, rods, and other devices would automatically generate intermediate and final figures.[34] Later on, in conversations with Babbage, Ada no doubt heard about proposed refinements, including plans to have the Difference Engine print out, respond to fail-safe devices, and ring a bell to signal and correct alignment problems or cause the engine to stop. The printing portion was an extremely important part of Babbage's considerations, as Alan Bromley points out, since it would embody the concept of programming and was an important transition to the Analytical Engine.[35]

As Ada knew, the difference Engine that sat in Babbage's studio was not finally what Babbage had in mind. Parts were missing, to be perfected, about to be conceived. The extent of his constant tinkering may be inferred from the recent discovery of machine fragments on a farm in Australasia, of manuscripts in a New South Wales regional museum,[36] and of the engine drawings Bromley rediscovered at King's College, London. The Difference Engine in the London Science Museum, a replica of which sits in the Antique Calculator Collection at IBM in New York—a brass rectangle, two-and-a-half feet by two feet—is only a model of what Babbage had in mind. Babbage argued in *Passages* and elsewhere that his original application to the government in April 1823 had been for a machine that would do both *"calculating* [of any function having a constant second difference] and *printing,"* which included setting type for printing the tables; and that Parliament had approved a two-part experiment, based on recommendations of the Royal Society for funding a full-scale model, one that would supposedly have run to dimensions of approximately ten feet by ten feet by five feet. This was not the general understanding, however, and by 1834, when Ada saw not only the Difference Engine but plans for the analytical machine, relations between the inventor and Lord Melbourne's government, already strained, were degenerating. In 1830, Babbage had written the rather sensational *Reflections on the Decline of Science in England and On Some Of Its Causes,* a tract reflecting his own frustrations but also the frustrations of those about to inaugurate the British Association. In words that would later be used in praise of his "interpret*ress"*—that she understood his Analytical Engine in all its "difficult and abstract" senses—Babbage had declared in *Reflections* that England was below other nations in respect of the "difficult and abstract sciences." *Reflections* proposed reforms and made enemies for him such as William Whewell and George Biddell Airy, both well connected with the government. Eight years later, in 1842, when Peel asked Airy (then astronomer royal) to give an opinion on the Analytical Engine, Airy replied: "Worthless." The astronomer Richard Sheepshanks, another enemy, was even nastier several years later, indicting Ada as well: Babbage couldn't be bothered explaining his own machine, Sheepshanks sneered, leaving the matter to a foreign mathematician [Menabrea] and an English countess! It was a more cutting remark than calling Ada, Byron's daughter, insinuating as it did that Babbage was a hopeless dilettante and Lady Lovelace a bored amateur. To some extent, however, Sheepshanks was correct in his assessment. On November 3, 1842, Peel formally severed all connection with Babbage and his engines, having taken nine years to reply to Babbage's specific request for approval.

Babbage had been working on a model of the Difference Engine since 1822 and publishing accounts since June of that year, when he delivered a paper on the engine to the Astronomical Society. Years and pounds later (both his own money and

Parliament's), nothing much had changed. The Difference Engine was the "largest Government-sponsored research project of the time,"[37] and, for Babbage, extremely frustrating. Details of his agonizing and often absurd conflicts over ownership of tools with his engineer, the brilliant and erratic Joseph Clement, who several times made off with Babbage's drawings, occupy extensive sections in Babbage biographies. They could also constitute a short course in law. By 1834, the public was confused by or had become indifferent to further engine plans, content with the handsome mechanism that entertained, along with the Silver Lady, at the Dorset Street soirées.

Babbage was never at a loss to promote his engines, when he chose to, but he chose at significant times not to, leaving the way clear for the likes of Lardner to explain the Difference Engine, and Menabrea and Ada to explain the Analytical Engine. So long as Babbage went on modifying designs, he was reluctant, he said, to provide extensive explanation and illustration, wary of appearing to have completed his plans, which he felt he could not yet do. To borrow a term from W. H. Auden, Babbage had a "neural itch" ("overambition" is Bowden's word), a dis-ease which was growing increasingly expensive and self-threatening. Indeed, in 1836, Mrs. Somerville wrote to Ada that the machine would be the death of Babbage, "for certain I am that the human machine cannot stand that restless energy of mind." Babbage was obsessed. If calculation could be made to six decimal places, why not twenty? If a method worked according to a second order of differences, why not a sixth? Such an extended machine would have cost a fortune, of course, and required about two tons of brass, steel, and pewter clockwork, made to gauged standards with tools that also had to be made to specification.[38] The year Ada met Babbage, he was spending most of his time inventing notation systems and modifying engineering details, getting tools made, and securing workspace. In 1839 he would resign the prestigious Lucasian Chair in mathematics, at Cambridge, to work on his engines. The fact that Dionysius Lardner, not he, was giving general lectures on the Difference Engine suited him.

Babbage's own explanations of his engines, written from a distance of twenty years, are essentially two chapters in *Pas-*

sages, that informative but erratic *apologia pro vita sua,* more anecdotally political than consistently expository. The section on the Difference Engine concludes with bittersweet whimsy. Babbage shows frustration at not having been understood. He has just been asked a "remarkable" (read "ignorant") question: "Pray, Mr. Babbage, can you explain to me in two words what is the principle of this machine?" Babbage says he wishes the "querist had possessed a moderate acquaintance with mathematics," for he would have answered in four words, "The method of differences," or with a formula. One reason Babbage may have been particularly pleased with Ada's annotation of the Analytical Engine was that he could no longer tolerate such inquiries. He conceded in *Passages* that a mathematical answer to the remarkable question would have been "unintelligible" to those who asked the question in the first place. But he also knew that he had to depend on such people for support.

Babbage's sly watch for engine observers at his studio suggests that the gentleman with the "remarkable" question recorded in *Passages* was not unique. Once, Babbage recalls, he saw two men looking at his engine with intelligence, neither one English—a not too guarded criticism of his country's lack of appreciation. There were high-placed exceptions from time to time: the duke of Wellington, whose support was valuable but who was not always in office; the duke of Somerset; and Prince Albert, a few years later. The anecdote in *Passages* must have been based on fact, even though Babbage elfishly says that two other "remarkable" questioners turned out to be a member of the Upper House and a member of the lower. Babbage's final response to basic questions about the Difference Engine, however, shows his hurt and disappointment: "I am not able rightly to apprehend the kind of confusion of ideas that could provoke such a question" about how the machine handled wrong figures. Babbage simply could not make himself understood.

It must have been a great pleasure for him if someone sought him out at his soirées to ask intelligent questions. He certainly had enough of the other kind. As Harriet Martineau observed,

> His patience in explaining his machine in those days was really exemplary. I felt it so, the first time I saw the miracle, as it

appeared to me; but I thought so much more, a year or two after, when a lady, to whom he had sacrificed some very precious time, on the supposition that she understood as much as she assumed to do, finished by saying, "Now, Mr. Babbage, there is only one thing more that I want to know. If you put the question in wrong, will the answer come out right?" [This is the very same exchange Babbage records in *Passages* for the MPs.] All time and attention devoted to lady examiners of his machine, from that time forward I regarded as sacrifices of genuine good nature.[38]

Ada Lovelace came along at the right psychological time for Charles Babbage. As Hyman writes, "When so few cared about his engines, and fewer still understood them in the slightest degree . . . [her] combination of intelligent interest and charm was seductive."[40] Years later, in *Passages*, Babbage took as an epigraph for his chapter on the Analytical Engine a line from Byron's 1819 poem *Prophecy of Dante*: "Man wrongs, and time avenges." For Babbage, it was not to be for many years. For Ada, almost totally invisible for one hundred years, the wait would be much longer.

[CHAPTER 4]

Byronic
Counterforces

Not surprisingly, Ada absorbed a good deal of her mother's attitude toward mathematics. "God always acts Geometrically" had been the motto of Isaac Barrow (Newton's teacher), and mathematics was still thought of in the early nineteenth century as part of a Platonic tradition, a view that dominated the curriculum and the Senate House examinations at Cambridge. Mathematics, mainly geometry, was divine because it sought correspondences between the world of earthly measurement and the larger universe of unchanging forms and eternal time. The tradition invited missionary devotion and, among the more driven acolytes, a view of oneself as a priest—or priestess. Mathematics was sacred lore, to be pursued for the glory of a First Principle, or Principal. Long before irregular dosing on laudanum and claret would exaggerate her already emphatic prose, Ada Lovelace expressed a desire to serve in the temple of Hypatia. She had been educated to be disciplined by mathematics; now the discipline itself compelled her.

Although Ada began taking opium for an undiagnosed intestinal disorder, probably a couple of years previous to the writing of the "Notes," its effects operated on her differently at different times. A more likely source of Ada's sometimes hysterical expressions about serving God mathematically was a chemistry innately within—Byronic impulses—still driving her even after the "Notes" were completed. "I am simply the *instrument* for the divine purpose to act on & thro'," she wrote her mother in 1844.

"Like the Prophets of old, I shall *speak the voice* I am inspired with. . . . I may be the Deborah, the Elijah of Science, submitting to God & His agents to be used as their *"vocal* organ for the ears of mortals. . . ." She was a *Prophetess,"* she announced, supremely devoted to the *"One,"* whose essence she defined mathematically as "the great All-knowing Integral!"[1] Hyperbolic, to be sure, but consistent with sentiments that had begun to obsess her three years earlier and that may have owed their origin to a lifetime of Lady Byron's programming.

Indeed, it was a desire for mathematical glory, rather than a particular kind of mathematics, that compelled Ada. Seven years after seeing plans for the Analytical Engine and only one year before starting on the translation and "Notes," she was writing passionately, but still vaguely, about making her mathematical mark. She continued sending problems to Dr. King, to De Morgan, to Mrs. Somerville, and to Babbage, but what distinguishes the letters now, in 1841, is their explicit yearning. She makes vows. Theological overtones are apparent in the "Byronic" letter she sends Woronzow Greig in May 1841, which prompted him to advise care. Three months earlier, in a note to Babbage, a religious metaphor undercut by wit enforces her entreaty that he visit. She writes of celebrating the "Sabbath *Mathematically,* in one way or other." The date is February 22, 1841, and she is expecting the De Morgans on Sunday evening, but if they do not come, could he? She hopes to see him as soon as possible. She has been working "very strenuously" since she saw him last, and "successfully," especially "studying attentively the *"Finite Differences,"* a subject in which she has a "more particular interest, because I know it bears directly on some of *your* business."[2] What she wants, of course, is that his business should become her business. She dwells on their possible—nay, *"probable,"*—association, anticipating in such a relationship the answer to something she has *"long"* entertained, though in a "vague and crude form." The Analytical Engine is no doubt in her thinking, though nothing specific is mentioned. Instead, the letters from this period, the early 1840s, show her questing for a noble cause. "I think I am more determined than ever in my future plans; and I have quite made up my mind that nothing must be suffered to interfere with them." This, from the mother of three small children, the wife of the lord lieutenant of Surrey, and the apparent administrator of several households.

She announces to Greig that she is "going on *most excellently*," but that more can be expected since she has made an important decision. Mathematics would be the "occupation for a life-time. I consider it now as being, if I may so speak, my *Profession*." It was an interesting word, still used then, in the first half of the nineteenth century, in its original sense of professing faith. "Anything I may hereafter *do* or *accomplish*, will be doubtless if not immediately & directly connected with it, yet in some way centered upon it."[3] She has been thinking about this idea for the last six months, she adds, a period which brings her to the time shortly after the birth of her third child, Ralph. For the while, however, she will lay out "capital" for distant returns, a "glorious speculation." Similar language marks the letter to Sophia De Morgan (a not uncommon occurrence in a prolific correspondent), but to Greig, she rolled on with fevered energy: "You think I have powers; and you are right. But I know *myself* much; and I know that whatever powers I may have *now*, I shall have tenfold those powers at 60, with the measures I am taking." Like Keats, Ada hoped for a certain number of years to refine her God-given talents; and, like Keats, she would underestimate the time allotted to her. Unlike Keats, however, she never submitted to controlled apprenticeship or rigorous self-examination, though she repeatedly declared to her various correspondents that that was exactly what she had been doing.

The perceptive and conventional Greig was worried, not just for Ada's sake but for that of his good friend, Lord Lovelace, her somewhat dull but conscientious husband, who ten years later would be horrified on discovering the extent of his wife's overreaching. Greig cautioned Ada to go with God. She did, but in a way he had not intended. Patience and moderation do not seem to have been Lady Lovelace's strong suits. She feels, she writes Greig in 1841, as though "Heaven has given . . . [her] a mission"—a peculiar "*intellectual-moral* mission to perform." Two months earlier, in March, she wrote to Sophia about Frend's recent death, and about death in general, but then she continued in another vein—about joining a "high & deep *knowledge & philosophy*" to her own "peculiar temperament and instincts," and gaining the "philosophy, the training, the [mathe-matical] instrument" necessary for the realization of great plans."[4] The expressions must have confirmed for Sophia the vanity she had ascribed to the daughter of her selfless friend Lady Byron. Perhaps Ada sensed the odd impression her emo-tional declarations could sometimes make. She trusted that Sophia would not think her "enthusiastic, or imcomprehensi-ble." (Sophia did.) To Babbage, in the fall of 1839, she had been defensive on this score: "Do not reckon me conceited for I am sure I am the last person to think over-highly of *myself.*" She believed, however, that she could go far, given her "decided" taste, her *"passion,"* and her "native Genius" [talent].

Ada had begun pursuing Babbage with a pluckiness that must have been charming to him. She was aimless, but talented and sincere. While not jumping immediately at her offers of assist-ance, begun in 1836, Babbage had been encouraging. Her taste for mathematics was "so decided," he had written, that "it ought not to be checked."[5] She persisted, through pregnancies. By 1840, her third and last child born, she was writing to Babbage about finding the right sort of tutor, that *"Man"* to teach her successfully. By January of the next year she was ready to show Babbage a "certain book called my Mathematical Scrap-book." And she was ready, also, to have him put her "in possession of the main points relating to . . . [his] engine."[6] One week later, she timidly insists on a commitment: "I scarcely dare so exalt myself as to hope, however humbly, that I can ever be intellectually worthy to attempt serving *you.*" Within two years, however, she obviously found herself worthy enough to lecture Babbage on humility. Her own "uncompromising principle" had always been "to endeavour to love *truth & God before fame & glory,* or *even just appreciation,*" she scolds. His, on the other hand, has been to love *"fame, glory, honour yet more."* She is not *"blaming,"* only pointing out truths, without denying, inciden-tally, that such a characteristic could even be said to be a *"noble and beautiful* fact." Then, as though catching her Byronic mask in a mirror of truth, she adds, "Far be it from *me* to disclaim the influence of *ambition and fame.* No living soul ever was more imbued with it than myself. . . ." Indeed, the very same week she was writing to Lady Byron about her resolve to develop

God's truth for the use of mortals—and to leave a name.[7] Babbage was one of the rare few treated to Ada's ironic self-deflations.

There were, of course, duties she had to attend to, having to do with household and children, and social obligations. These she performed, but in an increasingly perfunctory manner. She was aware of her tendency to let domestic matters slide. Lord Lovelace made the best of her distractions, but then he had the aid of his ever-present mother-in-law, who was used to taking charge, now of his children. Unlike the extraordinary Mrs. Somerville, who seemed to have balanced demands of muse and family, Ada was becoming more consumed by other interests and frustrated by lack of work time. Her affection for her husband and children was genuine; it was rather that her passions lay elsewhere. They were passions, also, in the old sense of the word as "suffering." Her statements of dedication sound at times painfully devotional. In the January 1841 letter she wrote to Lady Byron about mathematics being a "serious pursuit," she also spoke of its being full of difficulty, but "the less immediately inviting the subject, the more doggedly does that large Concentrativeness of mine, backed by Firmness, set about the matter. . . ."[8] She had "some hard & dry work & *much* of it before . . . [her]," she acknowledged, but she was ready. The Spartan votiveness must have pleased Lady Byron, who would withhold pain-killing opium from her daughter eleven years later because suffering was good for the soul.

It was in 1841 too that Ada wrote to the electrician and inventor Andrew Crosse about his work in electro-crystallization and about her own disposition to try experiments. Could Crosse get her "constantly acting batteries?" She would explain: "Our family are an alternate stratification of poetry and mathematics." It was now her turn. Just months earlier she had sent a note to her mother, playfully speaking of playing off mathematics and music: "You will perceive that Mathematics are now getting up in the world. Operas for 4 months in the year, and Mathematics for 8, will do . . . well and help each other on very easily."[9] Lady Byron would have preferred an even greater tipping of the scales, absorbing as she did prevailing religious scruples about "the stage." Byron had had strong theatrical attachments, both to the theater and to some of its stars.

Ada, however, was expressing dedication not just to mathematics. In the same letter to her mother in which she announces gaining "strength of head & attention" from her love of mathematics, she says she also feels an "immense development of *imagination;* so much so, that I feel no doubt if I continue my studies, I shall in due time be a *Poet.* This effect may *seem* strange, but it is not strange to *me.*" And then, in an enigmatic line, never explained, that must have given Lady Byron pause, Ada adds, "I believe I see its causes & connection clearly." She is giddy with excitement. A wonderful "exhilaration of spirits" and "deep confidence" move her. She feels she will "add to the accumulated & accumulating knowledge of the world," keeping glory a secondary consideration, of course. Within months, however, the wife of the earl of Lovelace would also be declaring an undying love for dramatics and music and thinking about these for a career. The world's "first computer programmer," then, had not clearly set about focusing her energies on Babbage's engine; indeed, the actual "program," the Bernoulli numbers expansion she was to explore in "Note G," seems to appear from out of nowhere.

Ada's passion for mathematics was genuine, though it was not as persistent as she wanted to believe—or as exclusive. She seems unaware of how her changed moods were sometimes responses to news about her famous father. In February 1841, Lady Byron, in Paris, sent Ada quite a letter. It contained Lady Byron's statement that Medora Leigh might well be Byron's illegitimate child by Augusta. Ada's written response, one month later, defensively refers only to Byron's "misused" talent: "If he has transmitted to me any portion of that genius, I would use it to bring out great *truths & principles.* I think he has bequeathed this task to me. I have this feeling strongly; & there is a pleasure attending it."[10] Whispers down corridors of time and across continents were one thing, but to receive, finally, such revelations from one's own mother about one's father was quite another. "Poor thing!" Lady Byron wrote. "You have a right to the excitability which appeared in you so early." Lady Byron had counted on mathematics to counteract that tendency, but what was happening was something unforeseen by Lady Byron and not fully understood by Ada: Ada's pursuit of mathematics would increasingly take on Byronic overtones, and, lacking a proper "Man" to guide her consistently, she would veer off competitively into other directions and restlessly, toward other men.

The year 1842 was particularly critical. Early in the year, Lady Byron was ensnared in the worst of Medora's machinations in Paris, sordid entanglements which Lady Byron believed it was her duty to superintend and, if possible, unravel. Sent periodic and detailed descriptions of these complicated and painful activities, Ada was at first depressed to the point that she could not study, but slowly, that spring, she recovered enough to announce new plans, though what they were strains the sense of recovery.

To her husband, she writes that she has great resources hidden beneath the surface. She must therefore try out different subjects to see what she will be best at, what will be permanent. She would, however, need to get away for contemplation. For the first time in a long while, she tells Lovelace, she feels *"stability"* of mind. But what she went on to declare to the socially circumspect earl must have struck him as just the opposite. She is thinking of studying "poetry, in conjunction with *musical composition.*" It *"must* be my destiny," poetry of a *"unique"* kind, more *"philosophical* & higher in it's [sic] *nature* than aught the world has perhaps yet seen."[11] Of course, she reasons, a careful apprenticeship will be necessary to achieve this goal, but it is apprenticeship in life that she has in mind. She has to *"see"* much, *"think"* much, *"study"* much, understand life in every phase and cultivate all the arts of expression *"practically"*—this word gets double underlining. But she can do it, she assures her husband. She knows she can write because she has indeed already written, and with "great facility." She sends along proof, something she did the other day suggested by a German balled of Schiller—not quite a translation but *"entirely different"* from the original. She feels now that her real talent is emerging: poetry. And she fears that her husband may check her; she hopes not. *"Just now"* she cannot bring herself to attend to science at all, meaning *"abstract"* [double underlining again] science. But "years only" will tell whether science "will be eventually merely my *subsidiary,* tho' profitable, amusement & relief from other pursuits; or whether it will in the end be in any way my *principal* & *grande* object." For the present, she must first give scope to her "*Dramatic* and *Expressive* tendencies." Lord Lovelace had obviously conveyed concern about her apparent abandonment of mathematics. What to say to Wheatstone and others about his wife's withdrawal from science? (Wheatstone would soon urge Ada to do the Menabrea translation.) Ada had an answer: she would explain her "slackened *scientific* energies" on grounds of health or medical injunction!

She realizes that she must appear "fickle," but William is not to worry: she is not under the influence of any mania. The more she strove to explain, however, the more she did not clarify. The fact is, she says, she's been studying herself and wants to pursue what she believes is "*pointed out & indicated by nature*" to best ensure her health and happiness, whatever that is, and it may not be science. Disturbing enough, but what did William make of her remarkable closing? Despite everything she's just written, she adds, she's aware of the nature of "*hysterical* consti-tutions" like hers, and so she distrusts all conclusions. It was not exactly a letter guaranteed to soothe fears. The hyperbole would grow stronger the following year.

To Andrew Crosse, she expressed great confidences about pursuing both science and music:

> You know I believe no creative ever could WILL things like a *Byron*. And perhaps that is at the bottom of the genius-like tendencies in my family. We can throw our *whole life* and *existence* for the time being into whatever we *will* to do and accomplish. You know perhaps the family motto, "*Crede Byron*". I think it not inappropriate, and especially when united with that of the Kings, "*Labor ipse voluptas*" [work itself is pleasure]. Now as I have married that motto, both *literally* and in my whole ideas and nature, I mean to do *what I mean to do*.[12]

She meant it "in *very* deed," because she quoted the family motto again in a similar letter to Babbage. She had also written to Crosse that for her the intellectual, moral, and religious life were all one, and that reading mathematics would be re-reading "God's natural works." She would "obey," she would "follow." But what she said she would follow was not necessarily mathe-matics. In December, close upon the translation and "Notes," Ada had been trying to reassure Greig that she would excell in no more than two things: one was playing the harp and singing, which she linked. As for the other, "I am not dropping the *thread* of science, Mathematics etc. These may still be my ultimate vocation." But then again, it might be *"musical composition"* that she would pursue with an "undivided mind." Time would tell. The letter rambles. She is *"very well,"* she assures him, but there are "seeds of destruction within me. This I *know."* She recognizes she lacks *"all* ballast & steadiness" and concedes that she cannot regard her life or powers as "other than precarious."[13] That same month, December 1842, she began to draw up concise statements about "Mr. Babbage's engine." It would be a kind of mental exercise, she wrote, to strengthen the logical faculty that would, in turn, help her order statements relating to the troublesome Medora Leigh affair. Measuring her way back to a less volatile state, she would use mathematics to reassert the rational force. But the conflict about where mainly to place her energies was not over. She did attempt poetry. "The Rainbow," one of her sonnets, turns up in the manuscript collection in various copies and versions, along with an undated sheet bearing the columnar pencil scrawl: "Vengeance!" *The World."* "Poetry." What did Ada Lovelace really know about her father's world, the realm of poetry?

Sophia De Morgan noted in her memoirs that Byron's poems had been in Lady Byron's bookcase at Fordhook, that Lady Byron made "several attempts" to interest Ada in them, but that Ada "had *no* taste for poetry."[14] For Caroline Fox, there was similar recollection. Lady Byron had an edition of Byron's works in her library to which Ada had "free access," but in which, apparently, she had no interest.[15] Was it the *Collected Poems,* bound in yellow morocco that Hobhouse had given Lady Byron as a wedding gift? If so, then its date, 1815, means that it was hardly representative of the Byron canon. That both Sophia De Morgan and Caroline Fox felt it necessary to insist on Lady Byron's disinterested character suggests that there may have been reason to think otherwise. Byron's poetry was certainly available in the Milbanke-Byron household, but how much of it was read by Ada then or later on (libraries were restricted for young ladies in the Victorian period), and how openly, are questions that remain merely speculative.

From the time of the separation, England had divided into two camps, Byron's and Lady Byron's, as a war of words and legal machinations ensued that kept erupting well into the century and beyond. In 1869, the editors of the *Argosy* apologized for printing private material (Ada's letters to Andrew Crosse), even though, they said, it may be deemed that no apology would be necessary: "Byron, his wife, and all connected with them, have recently been made the property of the world for discussion and gossip. . . ."[16] Perhaps Lady Byron may not have been as receptive to Byron's poetry as Sophia De Morgan and Caroline Fox suggest, two ladies who had enlisted on Lady Byron's side. As Sophia noted in her Reminiscences, Lady Byron had once read some of Lord Byron's "beautiful minor poems" to Ada, who did not appreciate them.[17] Just as William Frend had referred to Byron's *Hebrew Melodies* but not *Childe Harold*, so his daughter and Caroline Fox may have recalled a bookcase of selected Byron works. After all, in 1830 Lady Byron had had to see a phrenologist for a third time because of the recent publication of Tom Moore's *Life of Byron* (which she said she had steadfastly refused to read). As to Byron's romantic Eastern tales and the Faustian dramatic poem *Manfred*, with their brooding villainous heroes, and the satiric *Don Juan*, especially the early cantos on Lady Byron—though masked, these were hardly unsuggestive of incest, dark deeds, and marital discord. If Lady Byron had urged Ada to read *this* poetry, it might well have been in order to elicit sympathy.[18] In any event, not until Ada was married and shown a manuscript of Byron's 1818 poem *Beppo*, by his publishers, had she even seen her father's handwriting.[19] And what, then, did she think? *Beppo* ("ENGLAND! with all thy faults I love thee still . . .") was a sarcastic put-down of things English by way of celebrating things Italian, mainly the sensual life. It was also only after Ada was married that she saw the famous open-shirt painting of her handsome father, done by Phillips. She had been encouraged to see Byron as a sentimental outlaw versifier, less sinned against than sinning, and to guard against such attractive influence. What better talisman than mathematics, especially as it was associated with logical processes and with high-born metaphysics?

In 1843, in a bold and confident mood as she was revising the "Notes," attending to minute details in revision, Ada proclaimed to Babbage that in a year or so, she expected to be *"really something of an Analyst."* The more she studied, she noted approvingly, "the more insatiable do I feel my genius [talent] for it to be." But that was not all: "I do *not* believe that my father was (or ever could have been) such a *Poet* as *I shall* be an *Analyst* (& Metaphysician), for with me the two go together indissolubly."[20] Her choice of words is significant.

The word *metaphysician* in the nineteenth century did not just mean philosopher; it also carried a connotation of otherworldliness. Ironically, the *Oxford English Dictionary* gives *Don Juan* as a source: "And he [Juan] . . . turned, without perceiving his condition, / Like Coleridge, into a metaphysician" (I, xci). The editor of the Norton critical edition of Byron's poetry observes that the line is part of a three-stanza group in which "Byron jokingly rehearses the great speculative themes of Romantic metaphysics—and attributes them all to adolescent sexual anxiety."[21] The remark is ironically suggestive: shortly after the birth of her daughter, Anne, Ada fantasized about her *"metaphysical"* child. "If she will only be kind enough to be a metaphysician & a mathematician instead of a silly minikin dangling *Miss* in leading strings I shall love her *mind* too much to care whether her *body* is male female or neuter." "All joking apart," Ada continued, there was something she could sense in her newborn daughter which had "nothing to do with her sex either way." So Ada expressed herself to Lady Byron in 1838.[22] In fact, Anne would become the most intellectually competent of the Lovelace children, the most like her mother. And her mother would soon deliver herself of another "child," who would impress critics as coolly masculine.

Although Ada seems not to have been self-conscious about being a woman studying mathematical science, a letter to Babbage in July 1843 suggests that she was aware of prevailing attitudes. She boldly describes her prose style as *"pithy & vigorous"* and *"most striking,"* and she adds that she discerns in it a *"half-satirical & humorous dryness"* which would make her "a most formidable *reviewer."* She was "quite thunder-struck" at the *"power"* of her writing, she went on. "It is especially unlike a *woman's* style surely but neither can I compare it with any *man's* exactly." During the same period, she also says, "To say the truth, I am rather *amazed* at them [the "Notes"] & cannot help being struck quite *malgre moi* with the really masterly nature of the style, & its superiority to that of the Memoir itself." Her "first child" was doing fine, and Lord Lovelace was also pleased "beyond measure" with the baby's *"learned and knowing aspect. . . ."*[23] Perhaps, then, it was not simply Victorian deference that prompted her to sign each note with initials. Manic declarations about strong style notwithstanding, Ada must have been aware of hostile attitudes toward women who wrote on mathematical science. Harriet Martineau recalled how Mrs. Somerville, once asked to ensure that the next edition of *On the Connection of the Physical Sciences* would be in popular and intelligible prose, replied that she could not at all see her way to modify in that direction. "The scientific mode of expression, with its pregnancy, its terseness and brevity, seemed to her perfectly simple. If she was to alter it, it could be only by amplifying; and she feared that would make her diffuse and comparatively unintelligible."[24] A masculine prose style meant that one would be taken seriously.

In 1845, Ada's name would be one of several mentioned as the possible author of a popular book, anonymously published and widely criticized—*Vestiges of the Natural History of Creation*, a sensational argument for deity by way of geology.[25] Lovelace told Hobhouse about the allegation over dinner, but anyone who had read both the book and the "Notes" would have seen a great difference in style. That Ada's name should even have been offered, however, suggests that the "Notes" had not been widely read. *Vestiges* had what the influential *Edinburgh Review* disparagingly called a "feminine" style, or so it seemed to the editors who damned the book with no faint praise. Sarcastically, they confessed to having speculated on the authorship and concluded it had to be female, "trac[ing] therein the markings of a woman's foot." Now they begged pardon of the sex for their presumption (having discovered, of course, that the author was Robert Chambers).

We were led to this delusion by certain charms of writing—by the popularity of the work—but its ready bounding over the fences of the tree of knowledge, and its utter neglect of the narrow and thorny entrance by which we may lawfully approach it; above all, by the sincerity of faith and love with which the author devotes himself to any system he has taken to his bosom. We thought no *man* could write so. . . . The ascent up the hill of science is rugged and thorny, and ill-fitted for the drapery of a petticoat.

Specifically, the *Edinburgh* editors attacked the predilection in the *Vestiges* for seeing similarities in events when science proceeds by "following out differences." In short, the editors concluded that the author of the *Vestiges* was ignorant of geology, astronomy, and, especially, the nature of argument: the book was "feminine" in the worst sense of the word.

Although "feminine" was how Albany Fonblanque described Ada's manners, tastes, and musical talent, in a memorial essay for the *Examiner*, he used the word *masculine* to praise the "solidity, grasp, and firmness" of her mathematical brain. "The superficial observer would never have divined the strength and the knowledge that lay hidden under the womanly graces," he declared in tribute.[26] The "Notes" are not mentioned, but Fonblanque no doubt knew about them from the fact that he was both an editor and a member of the same social circle. Hobhouse made similar observations on Ada's manner and style. Sitting next to her at dinner one evening at the Lovelace home (June 3, 1846), he noted that she "spoke very freely on subjects few men and no women venture to touch upon—e.g. she remarked that the common argument in favor of a future state derives from the pleasing hope, the fond desire, the longing after immortality—in which she did not believe." A year earlier, he obviously found it unusual enough to remark on her tendency to "weigh her words and speak deliberately."[27]

The mathematician-metaphysician-analyst connection could take hold with Byronic effects. Writing to Babbage that July as she was revising the "Notes," Ada described her *"brain"* as "something more than merely *mortal; as time will show; (if only my breathing* & some other etceteras do not make too rapid a progress *towards* instead of *from* mortality)"—an ominous postscript. Then there is a rush of rodomontade such as would have tantalized the author of *Manfred:* "Before ten years are over, the Devil's in it if I haven't sucked out some of the life-blood from the mysteries of this universe, in a way that no purely mortal lips or brains could do." She concludes with reference to an *"awful* energy & power" that lie "yet undeveloped" in her *"wiry* little system."[28] A few days later (July 10), again to Babbage, she writes, "I am working, very hard for you; like the Devil in fact; (which perhaps I *am*.)" Henry Acland might have smiled wanly had he heard her; Babbage's response might have been more thoughtful. Just a few days earlier, she had written him of her scheme to take on the universe.

I intend to incorporate with one department of my labours a complete reduction to a system, of the principles & methods of *discovery*, elucidating the same with examples. I am already noting down a list of discoveries hitherto made, in order myself to examine into their *history, origin, & progress*. One first & main point, *whenever & wherever* I introduce the subject, will be to *define* & to *classify* all that is to be legitimately included under the term *discovery*. Here will be a fine field for my *clear, logical & accurate,* mind, to work its powers upon; & to develop its *metaphysical* genius, which is not least amongst its qualifications and characteristics.[29]

Ada's linking of "mathematical," "analytical," and "metaphysical" also suggests that she may not have been as disposed as Babbage to the useful and the mechanical, which would not be surprising. She had been taught to value abstraction as a way of honoring God and virtue. The author of the *Argosy* article suggests that Ada's letters show a "comprehensive grasp of intellect," "noble sentiments," and "innate reverence for the Deity," as well as enthusiastic feelings for her father (interesting associations). Abstract mathematics could encourage purity of soul.

If God acted geometrically, He might act analytically as well, but not mechanically. Ada's grandiose plans reflect a striving to appear as a "pure" mathematician liberated from the world. The "Notes," a fortuitous convergence of need, talent, and chance, also purified Ada in another sense as well. She had bouts of great pain during their composition that July, was *"very* ill & harrassed," as she wrote Babbage. But she pushed on with queries about integrals and functions. Who knows what was wrong? Not Dr. Locock, though he seemed to be treating her correctly. It was an "anomalous affair Altogether," she mused, "A *Singular Function*, in very deed!"[30] But later on that month, to her mother, she wrote about her agony in quite a different spirit. She would be "perfectly content" if pain were "the necessary condition of all that wonderful & available mental power which I see grounds to believe I am acquiring. I conceive that my state of health is in the inevitable *condition* attached to the nature of my mind, & will never be an *impediment* to the development of this. . . ." She certainly picked the wrong one to whom to say, "Give me *powers* with *pain* a million times over, rather than *ease* with even *talents*. . . ."[31]

Lord Byron in Albanian costume, by Thomas Phillips, R.A., 1814, soon after Byron's fame for "Childe Harold's Pilgrimage, Cantos I and II." Courtesy of the National Portrait Gallery.

Lord Byron: an engraving, based upon six portraits. From top left down: by Kay, 1795; by Westfall, 1814; by Harlowe, 1817. From top right down: by Saunders, 1807; by Phillips, 1814; by Thorwalden, 1810. Courtesy of The New York Public Library, Manhattan division.

Ada, aged four, from a miniature in a locket sent to Byron by his sister. Courtesy of John Murray (Publishers) London.

Ada Augusta [sic], Countess of Lovelace, at age seventeen (1832). Lord Bowden thought this showed a distinct resemblance to Byron (See *Faster than Thought*). Courtesy of the Lovelace-Byron Collection.

Ada at twenty-seven in a traditional costume of the period. Sketch by A. E. Chalon (1780-1860), subject and portrait painter. Courtesy of John Murray (Publishers) London.

The 1835 portrait of Ada by Margaret Carpenter was commissioned by Lady Byron. Ada: "I conclude . . . [Mrs. Carpenter] is bent on displaying the whole expanse of my capacious jaw bone, upon which I think the word Mathematics should be written." October 29, 1835. Courtesy of the British Government Art Collection.

Ada in 1852 at the piano, painted by Henry Phillips, the son of Thomas Phillips, R. A. She was in great pain at the time but insisted on sitting for the son of the artist who had painted her father. Courtesy of Doris Langley Moore and John Murray (Publishers) London.

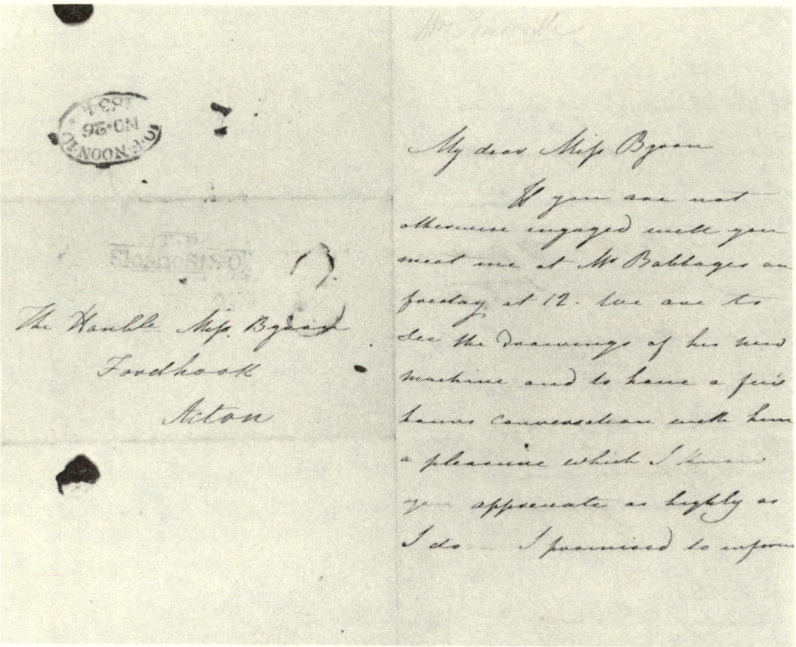

[Handwritten letter, partially legible]

My dear Miss Byron

If you are not otherwise engaged will you meet me at Mr Babbages on friday at 12. We are to see the Drawings of his new machine and to have a few hours conversation with him a pleasure which I know you appreciate as highly as I do — I promised to inform

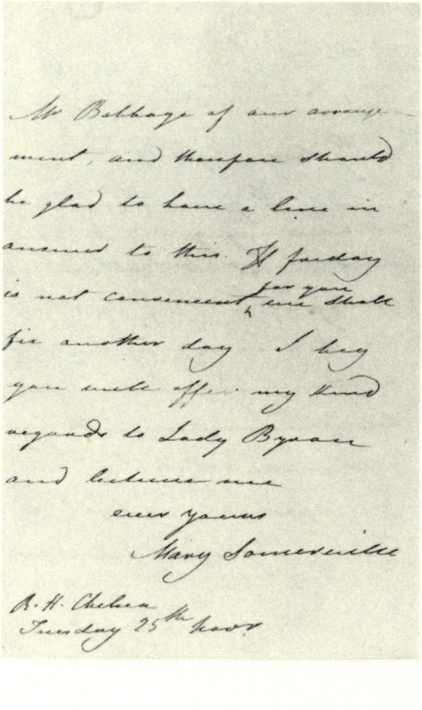

[Address panel]

The Hon'ble Miss Byron
Fordhook
Acton

[Continuation of letter]

Mr Babbage of our arrangement, and therefore should be glad to have a line in answer to this. If friday is not convenient for you we shall fix another day I beg you will offer my kind regards to Lady Byron and believe me

ever yours
Mary Somerville

C. H. Chelsea
Tuesday 25th Nov'r

This letter from Mary Somerville to Ada, written November 25, 1834, is as follows; "My dear Miss Byron If you are not otherwise engaged will you meet me at Mr Babbages on friday at 12. We are to see the Drawings of his new machine and to have a few hours conversation with him a pleasure which I know you appreciate as highly as I do. —I promise to inform Mr Babbage of our arrangement, and therefore should be glad to have a line in answer to this. If friday is not convenient for you we shall fix another day. I beg you will offer my kind regards to Lady Byron and believe me, ever your Mary Somerville." Courtesy of the Beinecke Rare Book and Manuscript Library, Yale University.

My Daughter! with thy name this song begun—
My Daughter! with thy name thus much shall end—
I see thee not—I hear thee not—but none
Can be so wrapt in thee—Thou art the Friend
To whom the Shadows of far years extend:
Albeit my brow thou never shouldst behold,
My voice shall with thy future visions blend
And reach into thy heart—when mine is cold,
A token and a tone even from thy father's mould.

(Above) From Lord Byron's manuscript of Canto III of "Childe Harold's Pilgrimage" (1816). The manuscript is from a large red notebook discovered, along with many other papers, in 1976, in a leather-studded chest at Barclays Bank, London. The opening line is addressed to Ada. Courtesy of Barclays and the British Library. *(Below)* Charles Babbage (1792-1871), from the *Illustrated London News*, November 4, 1871.

Model of The Difference Engine in the Antique Calculator Collection, IBM Gallery of Science and Art. Courtesy of the IBM Corporation, Armonk, New York. Photography by Jennifer Baum.

Model of The Analytical Engine in the Antique Calculator Collection, IBM
Gallery of Science and Art. Courtesy of the IBM Corporation, Armonk, New
York. Photography by Jennifer Baum.

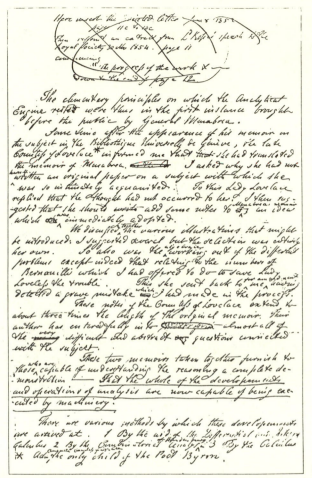

Babbage's crediting of Ada Lovelace's work in his autobiographical *Passages from the Life of a Philosopher* (1864). The relevant part reads: "Sometime after the appearance of his [Menabrea's] memoir on the subject in the Bibliothèque Universelle De Génèvre, the late Countess of Lovelace informed me that she had translated the memoir of Menabrea. I asked why she had not herself written an original paper on a subject with which she was so intimately acquainted. To this Lady Lovelace replied that the thought had not occurred to her. I then suggested that she should add some notes to Menabrea's memoir, an idea which was immediately adopted." In a footnote, Babbage identifies Ada as "the only child of the Poet Byron," which, at the time the notes were written, was true.

This manuscript is in the Wanganui Regional Museum in Auckland, New Zealand, and was brought to my attention by Professor Garry J. Tee of the department of computer science, University of Auckland. Courtesy of the Wanganui Regional Museum.

Augustus De Morgan photographed by Ernest Edwards in the mid-1860s.
Courtesy of the Tucker Collection, Science Museum Library, London.

The United States Department of Defense

Invites You to Attend the Debut

of the

Ada Programming Language

September Fourth and Fifth, Nineteen Hundred Eighty

U.S. Department of Commerce Auditorium

Constitution Avenue at Twelfth Street, N.W.

Presentation by Dr. Jean Ichbiah
(Principal Language Designer)

Starting at Nine o'Clock Each Morning

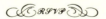

(Above) Ada, on her deathbed. The sketch was by, and is signed by, Lady Byron. Courtesy of the Lovelace-Byron Collection. *(Below)* Copy of the invitation sent out by the United States Department of Defense in introducing the Ada programming language and setting up Ada programming offices.

[CHAPTER 5]

The "Notes"

She called the "Notes" her "child," but the "uncommonly fine baby" was necessarily dependent on Menabrea to be born and on Babbage for delivery. The labor was intense but not protracted. The mother, exceedingly anxious about her child and not in the best of health, physical or mental, during the gestation period, "*will* have it *well* and *fully* done or not at all." She declares this as she shoots sections over to Babbage for correction and scolds him for his sloppiness. She is convinced, however, that her "child" will become a "*man* of the first magnitude and power."[1] What seems odd is that the "pregnancy" appears accidental. There was no mention of it until it was quite far along. Charles Wheatstone, who had suggested that Ada translate Menabrea for the Scientific Memoirs, apparently had no idea it would appear with an annotation three times as long as the article.

But the gestation had really begun earlier, three years before, in 1840 (Ada was twenty-five; little Ralph, her third and last child, was barely one year old). Babbage had left for Italy, on the invitation of his friend Giovanni Plana (1781–1864), to lecture at Turin on the Analytical Engine. The eminent group of geometers and engineers assembled there included L. F. Menabrea (1809–1896), a military engineer who in 1860 would become a general in Garibaldi's army and in 1867 prime minister of Italy. Predictably, Babbage had brought along just about everything: drawings, models, notebooks of notations, drafts, versions of plans, illustrations, and charts. It was enough to tax the stamina of the fifty-nine-year-old Plana, who Babbage expected would write up the lectures. Although Babbage would refer to Menabrea later on in *Passages* as a "highly valued friend," he may have been somewhat disappointed that Plana, the better-known mathematician, had not been the one to do the article. But Menabrea, an admirer of Mrs. Somerville, to whom he had written *"de haute estime,"* was a cautious writer who did not hesitate to send copy and questions to Babbage for correction.[2] Engineering details were his chief concern, because the Turin philosophers who had invited Babbage to speak had wanted to hear about the engine's "executive" power: how the machine would act on mathematical instructions. Ada's "Notes" would be more on the legislative features, concepts inherent in the engine, its mathematical principles, and even musings about the future, these last of primary interest to general readers today though they were side considerations for Ada, her major attention going to the programs, or "illustrations."

Ada's "Notes" are indeed notes and not a unified, sustained explanation about the Analytical Engine. The seven, labeled "A" to "G", are not consistent in topic or tone, though some themes recur. Ada put her mind to service for Babbage, but she also gave him something of her heart: she was genuinely concerned about his well-being, as was Lord Lovelace. The "Notes" never mention Babbage by name, but not primarily because Ada wanted to be clear of his quarrels. Rather, her main motive seems to have been to act protectively on his behalf, to keep the engine foremost in mind, not its "irrascible" inventor. The "Notes" reflect her sense that in order to win supporters, the Analytical Engine needed to be distinguished clearly from the earlier machine, the Difference Engine, now rejected by the government. Unfortunately, the general public, on whom much future support would depend, but presumably unsophisticated mathematically, would have found sections of the "Notes" forbidding, if not unintelligible.

Occasionally the prose hints at spiritual insularity: precise, abstract, formal, suggesting an intense student in an advanced mathematics class. At other times, the "Notes" soar, metaphysically, with the "prophetess" intuiting strange and powerful significances.

"NOTE A"

By choosing to begin the first note with remarks about the kind of mathematical function the Difference Engine was constructed to tabulate, Ada was moving from what was known about Babbage's engines to what was generally unknown. She seems to have wanted to broaden the idea of what was "useful" without appearing to disparage the earlier invention. The Difference Engine was an ingenious calculator, valuable but also limited. In order to present the Analytical Engine in all its complex and conceptual glory, Ada may have concluded that she first had to disabuse readers of false expectations and possible confusions. "No very clear or correct ideas prevail as to the characteristics of each engine," she writes. She will explain the difference, but it will be difficult in the small space she has at her disposal. The annotations, after all, were merely notes to someone else's article, and that in turn was not even written by the inventor.

The complication of the Analytical Engine came from Babbage's desire to do more with less, to make it elegantly simple. Simplicity has always been a hallmark of mathematical beauty, but it requires an educated mind and eye for appreciation. Arguing that Ada had no firm grasp of mathematics and suffered from "prophetic vagueness," Stein writes, "It was the formal beauty and surprising, seemingly magical results of mathematical processes and reasoning which entranced her."[3] Just so. It is rather what Stein disparagingly calls Ada's "essentially intuitive and mystical" disposition that has interested historians. The "Notes" were the timely accident of one driven to do mathematics by a mother who, far from encouraging fanciful tendencies, had done what she could to combat them.

Ada wanted to explain the Analytical Engine and also promote it. Two audiences are therefore addressed throughout the "Notes": "the public," and the specialists, whom Ada refers to from time to time as those with knowledge and training. Between the two, however, it was the specialists she primarily wrote for. "Note A" begins mathematically with the equation whose integral the Difference Engine was constructed to tabu-

late: $\Delta^7 u_x = 0$, the solution being $u_x = a + bx + cx^2 + \ldots + gx^6$.
With his eye primarily on mechanical features, Menabrea had
written that the Difference Engine gave rise to the Analytical
Engine, but Ada foresaw a likelihood that the Analytical Engine
would be seen as just a development of the earlier machine, so
that the crucial differences between them, actual and projected,
would not be appreciated: only the Analytical Engine was
capable of handling general information and could change during a given "program," written on punched cards. This difference between the engines is one that she returns to throughout
the thirteen-page note. She recognizes, she says, that there is
much "vagueness" and "inaccuracy" about the two engines.
What she did not say was that Babbage himself was responsible
for some of the confusion. He had refused to write fully about
the design or purposes of his engines, and when he did, years
later, it was to provide what might be called the "judicial"
explanation—his apologia, his sense of betrayal, his despair.
Vagueness also remained, however, because some of the problems Babbage was having with the engine did not yield to
solution. The opening idea, that a machine might be general in
its application and valuable primarily because it could stimulate
mathematical thinking, may also have given her pause. Was the
government likely to support a complicated machine whose
great attraction would be mainly for mathematicians? Both
machines would save time in doing arithmetic operations and
protect against errors inherent in human calculation, but to be
useful a machine did not necessarily have to serve only a
specific, practical purpose.

Intent on being an effective expositor, Ada provides compari-
sons, analogies, repetitions, examples, though today many of
these would not be considered proper style or form. She has
translated Menabrea, and rather than repeat his description, she
says, she would complement it by expanding and illustrating,
while she looks to someone like Dionysius Lardner to provide a
mechanical exposition. The Analytical Engine, she points out, is
a unique device which uses a system of controlling cards like
those used by the Jacquard loom in weaving brocaded silks. It is
not just another calculating machine, Ada stresses; it "holds a
position wholly its own"; its essence is an ability to be pro-

grammed, that is, to act on general instructions about the succession and distribution of general symbols in "unlimited variety and extent," even to change those instructions in mid-process.[4] Unlike the Difference Engine, the Analytical Engine was designed to "analyze" data, give orders about how to proceed, and do arithmetic in all four basic operations, though division would prove more problematic than Babbage had anticipated. In a footnote, Ada explains that the "operation" cards which instruct the Analytical Engine are "wholly independent of those cards which are used for other purposes," and are not tied to specific numerical data. This separation of functions, as historians of science point out, corresponds to de Prony's mathematical appropriation of Adam Smith's division of labor, the last two divisions being given over to the machine, the first one reserved to the "programmer." The separation thus represents the main advance of the Analytical Engine—its ability to respond to symbols, not just numbers. The conceiving of the formula belongs to the "programmer." It is he, not the machine, who originates everything, as Ada says in the last of the notes.

"Note A" has meaning for both specialist and general reader and is the most readable of the seven notes. Those who would have preferred the Silver Lady to the Difference Engine would have had little difficulty with most of its commentary. Particularly attractive for them would have been the analogy emphasizing the difference between Babbage's two machines, a speculation about computer music, and, later on, an impassioned statement about the meaning of mathematics. The analogy is often quoted in histories of science that include early work on computers. The Analytical Engine "*weaves algebraical patterns* just as the Jacquard loom weaves flowers and leaves," Ada wrote. (A recent French appreciation suggests that Ada should not have used the present tense of "to weave" because no analytical engine had been realized, a point that is sometimes forgotten by modern critics).[5] Earlier in "Note A" there is another apt analogy. The Difference Engine is to arithmetic as the Analytical Engine is to analysis (Ada's use of the word *analysis* here is in the sense of separation of a whole into its component parts, rather than in the French sense of the calculus). The Analytical Engine, she saw, was designed to break a complex problem into a series of smaller sequences or operations, an essential use of the computer today. Here was the key difference between the two engines. "The bounds of *arithmetic* were . . . outstepped the moment the idea of applying the [operation] cards had occurred." The idea is not explored in detail, but it contains important distinctions between the machines which Ada pursued elsewhere. The Difference Engine had to have some kind of pre-processing in order to get started: first numbers, data already computed, had to be set on the columns; the human mind had to do calculations. The Analytical Engine, on the other hand, did not require human intervention, because the operation cards would "mind" the sequences, so to speak.

But of course the Analytical Engine had no existence beyond drawings, and there was good reason, therefore, for the "misty notions" Ada claimed were held about the engine by both the "mathematical reader" and "the public."[6] There was another reason, however, why full explanation would be difficult, but Ada would not have mentioned it. How could one compare and contrast two engines, one of which had already cost the government a fortune, the second of which would never be built? She tried, but not just for Babbage's sake. Lady Lovelace also enjoyed the role of priestess.

As the requirements of science increase and the capabilities of the engine become better known, she continued in "Note A," the Analytical Engine will take on new powers. What shame if "some *other* nation or government" should realize the project and jeopardize "the honour of our country's reputation in the future pages of history." She appeals to that time: "A new, a vast, and a powerful language is developed for the future use of analysis, in which to wield its truths so that these may become of more speedy and accurate practical application for the purposes of mankind than the means hitherto in our possession have rendered possible." Computer music is also anticipated: "Supposing, for instance, that the fundamental relations of pitched sounds in the science of harmony and of musical composition were susceptible of such expression and adaptions, the engine might compose elaborate and scientific pieces of music of any degree of complexity or extent." Ada was apologetic about such speculations, however. Such wild "flights of fancy" were the hallmark of the popular science writer of the time,[7] as the *Vestiges* controversy revealed, and it was an image "A.A.L." would avoid. In 1837, Dickens had begun to parody such conjecturing in "The Mudfog Papers." Then, too, Ada must have known the Newtonian philosophical position: *non fingo hypotheses* ("I do not create hypotheses"), the watchwords of the *Optics* that had dominated Cambridge. However, as Newton himself and many natural philosophers afterwards had done, Ada, aware of the tradition, violated it.

The heart of "Note A" is philosophical. The main argument has to do with the engine's intellectual benefits. The Analytical Engine would be "useful," not just in doing what the Difference Engine could do but in advancing mathematical thinking by clarifying logical procedures. Ada was curious about what the rational process might appropriate from studying the discrete operations of the engine. She observed that "confusion," "difficulties," and "contradictions" arose from improper distinctions among operations (processes), objects (data), and their (numerical) results—features the Analytical Engine separated mechanically. Unknowingly, she was anticipating a division between logic and mathematics that would develop later on in the century. Knowingly, she was pointing out an important value of Babbage's machine: Not only could it help refine mathematical thinking, but it might also clarify notation, separating symbols used to signify operations from those representing quantities. This idea of a machine's apparent rational processes somehow clarifying human processes of thought is at the heart of artificial intelligence, the computer simulation of cognition—though to Ada, and even to the great inventor himself, just how the handling of symbols separate from number was to be effected mechanically is not clear. Perhaps Ada stumbled on the idea. But the fact is she observed, studied, questioned, and persevered enough to create in herself conditions for such musings.

She also foresaw that operation mechanisms could act on numbers and also on letters, and on whatever relations could be expressed symbolically, though this last explanation is somewhat murky, owing perhaps to inconsistency among the engine drawings she saw (Babbage had been reworking this feature for several years), and to the fact that no plan on paper could adequately illustrate how an operating mechanism would do algebraical calculations (the Bernoulli chart, in this regard, does not provide the answer). But she did see that the idea of using a symbolic representation for both processes and results, numerical and algebraic, was an important subject, one that had interested Babbage, Peacock, and Herschel since Analytical Society days; a subject that had not then met with sufficient attention or appreciation, as Anthony Hyman points out.[8]

"Note A," which delighted Babbage, seems to have had special meaning for Ada, who midway through decided to celebrate mathematics. In eloquent, perhaps religious, voice she sounds a transcendental theme that seems Euclidean in its correspondence at the same time as it suggests personal yearning. To Babbage, the author of the *Ninth Bridgewater Treatise*, one sentence in particular may have stood out. It may also have set a record for mathematical exposition: It is 158 words long.

> Those who view mathematical science, not merely as a vast body of abstract and immutable truths, whose intrinsic beauty, symmetry and logical completeness, when regarded in their connexion together as a whole, entitle them to a prominent place in the interest of all profound and logical minds, but as possessing a yet deeper interest for the human race, when it is remembered that this science constitutes the language through which alone we can adequately express the great facts of the natural world, and those unceasing changes of mutual relationship which, visibly or invisibly, consciously or unconsciously to our immediate physical perceptions, are interminably going on in the agencies of the creation we live amidst: those who thus think on mathematical truth as the instrument through which the weak mind of man can most effectually read his Creator's works, will regard with especial interest all that can tend to facilitate the translation of its principles into explicit forms.

Seen against such assumptions of power and glory, the Analytical Engine becomes a kind of holy instrument, an agent capable of translating the principles of Creation that man reads in the book of the universe; and because such translation is relatively error-free, the engine can be viewed as a reliable and valuable instrument. Babbage wrote that "Note A" was an admirable and philosophic view of the engine, and that Ada should not alter it.[9] Other notes, however, would cause her considerable concern, and pique at Babbage, because of his suggestion to delay publication. The period during which the "Notes" were composed and revised was clearly, for her, a time of enormous anxiety and physical and mental strain.

"NOTE B"

A more exacting section for the non-specialist, though only half the length of "Note A," "Note B" expands upon a concluding remark in the preceding commentary that "mechanism has undoubtedly gone much further to meet mathematics, in the case of this engine, than of the former one." "Note A" ends with an implicit challenge (or warning) to the general reader. Comparing Menabrea's "comprehensive and generalized memoir" on the Analytical Engine with Lardner's lecture on the Difference Engine, with its "moderate quantity of rather dry details," Ada states that the two pieces are "peculiarly valuable to each other; at least for the purposes of those who really desire something more than a merely superficial and popular comprehension of the subject of calculating engines."

Although "Note B" concentrates on explaining the "storehouse" columns (the memory containers) on the Analytical Engine, at least two hundred as compared with seven for the Difference Engine, the note is of main interest today for its modern-day correspondences. By way of a diagram, Ada describes the use of certain boxes as a kind of memorandum space for the observer, to show what is going on." This notation in no way influences processes or results," she adds, suggesting to a modern reader that the notation was like REM (remark or comment) statements today, non-executable lines a programmer writes that mark what is being done at what stage.

"Note B" gave Ada headaches. It was "plaguing her to death" she wrote Babbage, close to the publication deadline. She was "beside [herself] with hurry and work." Making minor alterations demanded "minute consideration and many nice adjustments." Too bad Babbage was not as "accurate" and anticipatory of difficulties as she.[10] Indeed, his "wrong references and blunderations" made a mess of her phrasings and sentences. Still, no special thanks to him, she imperiously adds, "Note B" is "excellent." She was often given to favorable self-evaluations and he almost always agreed, but approval usually followed numerous exchanges of letters, prompted by Ada's anxiety to understand and get details correct.

The heart of "Note B" is the explanation of the difference between cards that determine operations for the adding states or multiplying states in the "mill" (the calculating portion), and cards that distribute the operations according to a particular function, feeding the mill with the proper "food" and receiving the results. Everything is registered on columns of disks and gears. Ada says she must avoid getting into minutiae, because of the limits of space, but in the interests of accuracy, she does mention special conditions under which a "programmer" might have difficulty. The note stays with main ground, however, such as the engine's ability to store intermediate results as well as final calculations or combined ones. This feature is very much at the heart of modern-day computing.

"Note B" concludes on the same theme as "Note A": the ultimate benefit of the engine to clear thinking: "The further we analyse the manner in which such an engine performs its processes and attains its results, the more we perceive how distinctly it places in a true and just light the mutual relations and connexion of the various steps of mathematical analysis; how clearly it separates those things which are in reality distinct and independent, and unites those which are mutually dependent."

"NOTE C"

This, the shortest note of the seven, begins with reference to the London Polytechnic Institution and the Adelaide Gallery. The Adelaide Gallery of Practical Science (named for the consort of William IV, the same Queen Adelaide at whose ball Ada had met Babbage in 1833) had been opened in 1832 for the exhibition of models of inventions, works of art, and specimens of novel manufacture. The Polytechnic Institution was opened in 1838 to advance the arts and the practical sciences. Both galleries reflected a growing interest in science, an absorption with applications and mechanisms, and the increasing presence of women. At the Polytechnic, Babbage heard lectures on the diving bell, and Ada may well have seen a Jacquard loom on display there, though she does not specifically mention it.

"Note C" contains certain details about the Analytical Engine that could only have come from frequent discussions with Babbage. Babbage had been working on a method he called "backing"—making cards revolve backwards instead of forwards "at pleasure" in order to achieve iteration by the simplest means. "The object of this extension was to secure the possibility of bringing any particular card or set of cards into use *any number of times successively* in the solution of one problem"—like a do-loop, or like a subroutine (a separate but related section of code) that has been called for in a specially devised program.[11] Backing had been "alluded to by M. Menabrea," Ada writes, but she would like to fasten on the process as "a very important simplification"—the use of just a few cards to weave symmetrical patterns. Such compression is at the heart of computing. Another advantage Ada saw in backing was what she had embodied in her weaving analogy in "Note A": exploring the patterns of *"intersecting threads"* could yield ideas for *"algebraical combinations."* And so the ultimate theme of "Note A" is sounded again in "Note C": the Analytical Engine is "useful" to advance mathematical thinking.

"NOTE D"

This note also brought a compliment from Babbage. He was very pleased with it, he said. "It is in your usual clear style and requires only one trifling alteration which I will make." The slight correction was owing, he pointed out, to "our not having yet had time to examine the outline of the mechanical part." Surely the pronoun "our" was gracious, but it reflected an attitude Babbage made clear in his Turin lectures: facing questions or statements about his own ideas, he often learned that he had to modify those ideas. He was always generous with associates: they gave him an opportunity to clarify his work and thus improve it. Although he was too busy to superintend every detail of Menabrea's and Ada's work, the record shows that he responded to their numerous inquiries for clarification.

There were three kinds of variable cards used, he wrote Ada in reference to "Note D," and he briefly described them. He would also like to omit one paragraph—he's marked it in pencil—and he's busying himself with some other mathematical matters. "Note D" needed clarifications, but he tripped lightly with her. He knew she was close to exhausting herself. Letters from her that July and August of 1843 were filled with news about her being ill, but she could still be playful: "It must be a very pleasant and merry sort of thing to have a *fairy* in one's service (minus limbs?). I envy you." She had only *"mortals"* to wait on her![12] Sometimes, however, she was not amused. In response to some of Babbage's emendations to "Note D," she wrote back annoyed and probably somewhat embarrassed, even though the corrections were but "trifling" alterations. She indicates slight alterations of her own that she meant to make in another note. She is the honor student, eager to please. She is also the neophyte, determined to be on her own and to be "somewhat" anonymous.

"Note D," detailed and complicated, and related to the abstruse "Note G" on the Bernoulli numbers, may be of interest only to specialists, but its territory is clearly where Ada saw her reputation to lie. The "public" is acknowledged, but it is the mathematicians, "at least," as "Note A" declared, whom she would have as her main readership. Her occasional arrogant response to Babbage's criticism reveals an anxiety related to the famous "temper" Byron intimated might be less Byron than Milbanke. But the "Notes" themselves are even-tempered, cool even to a fault, generous to Menabrea and somewhat self-effacing. In "Note D" Ada refers to her diagram of the variable columns of the engine as "merely another manner of indicating the various relations denoted in M. Menabrea's table." But she is pleased enough with her own efforts to declare that Menabrea's table and her diagram, combined, "form a complete and accurate method of registering every step and sequence in all calculations performed by the engine." At this point, she concedes (with pride, it may be assumed) that the discussion would be apparent only to "a mind somewhat accustomed to trace the successive steps by means of which the engine accomplishes its purposes"—that is, a mathematical mind. "It must be evident how multifarious and how mutually complicated are the considerations which the working of such an engine involve." Several distinct "sets of effects" go on simultaneously, independent yet exerting a mutual influence. She wishes she had more space to explain, but it was just as well she did not have. Even as she wrote, Babbage was advancing his design.

"NOTE E"

This trigonometrical note gave Ada particular trouble, but she writes to Babbage that no one "but me would have doggedly stuck to it, as I have been doing, in all its wearing minutiae."[13] Now again she illustrates the distinction made in "Note A" between arithmetic power and the algebraic power of the Analytical Engine. Working with trigonometric functions, she sets out to demonstrate how the Analytical Engine calculates a function containing variables. She finds slight discrepancies in Menabrea's data and makes corrections. Why, then, did she not correct the obvious error of a trigonometric function being misused for a word—"cos" for "cas"? The mistake had appeared in the Menabrea article [*Cependant, lorsque le cos. de* n = ∞". . .] Could Menabrea himself have made such an error? Could the French printer be at fault? Should not Menabrea have caught the error, or Ada, who did the translation twice, or Babbage, whom Ada asked to go over the revise carefully? There is no answer. A hectic exchange of pre-publication notes between Babbage and Ada, Ada signing herself in one of them "Addlepate," suggests that the error may have been overlooked in the frenzied correction and confusion of original material, revises, and proofs. In Menabrea's account (in French) cosine is abbreviated throughout without the period, except in the passage in contention where it is "cos." Stein declares that Ada's failure to correct the printer's error is prime evidence of the "tenuousness with which she grasped the subject of mathematics." Yet Menabrea's "cos." with the period was not commented on by Babbage, Taylor, Somerville or De Morgan, or by Lord Bowden who corrected the error but gave no explanation, and there is no reason to suggest that what for them is allowed to be oversight must be interpreted for Ada as "most telling and consequential" evidence of ignorance. Of course, Ada should have corrected the error. She certainly would have known that cosines can never have a value greater than one, and she most certainly recognized the sense of the passage she was translating: namely the ability of men over machines to "foresee" that as the numbers in a certain mathematical expression grow very large, approaching infinity, the calculated value of such an expression would approach *pi*, and computation would be impossible. Who knows why Ada did not see the mistake and correct it (though the double fault of vowel and punctuation error ("cos.") may have caused her not to feel the force of a word here. Regardless, it seems difficult to credit the charge that a printer's error in someone else's article, and occasional youthful outbursts of frustration at arithmetic (these surely not beyond the experience of working mathematicians), constitute irrefutable evidence of an adolescent mind getting by on rush and dazzle. Whatever the reason for the error (and Stein is indeed the first one to notice it), its presence in the translation need not adversely affect contemporary interest and admiration.

"Note E" emphasizes the versatility of the Analytical Engine and suggests, in its brief description of operation cards which designate cycles, modern-day function keys. Ada offers a complicated illustration, adding that it will be intelligible only if the reader understands "what is meant by an *n*th function" and recognizes the notation of integral calculus. However, "we have not space to give any preliminary explanations." So much for the general public courted in "Note A," although some of the emphases here will be familiar to beginning students of computing: the use of index "statements," and the anticipation of do-loops (iterations) and conditional responses (if this, then that).

"NOTE F"

This is a practical note, giving examples of how the engine would do difficult problems without error and reduce the number of needed cards for cycles. Only three operation cards would be needed to go through 330 operations to eliminate nine variables in ten equations, she explains. And only the same three would be necessary for thousands, even millions, of operations in simple equations of the same form. Probably from discussions with Babbage, Ada was able to provide evidence of discrepancies in astronomy tables, examples that proved the need for an engine to reduce calculation time and error. Such is the power of the engine that once the general algebraic form is set, the mere number is incidental, if the engine has sufficient memory of course.

"Note F" also speculates on the eventual solution of many problems now considered impossible because of "great expenditure of time, labour and money." Thus the machine "may prove highly important for some of the future wants of science, in its manifold, complicated and rapidly-developing fields of inquiry. . . ." Then, in a striking conjecture, Ada wonders if the engine might not be set to investigate formulas of no apparent practical interest. For example, a formula might be discovered to generate only primes. In this sense, she felt, the Analytical Engine could be used, as computers are used today, to find problems rather than to solve them. This speculation, the final thought of "Note F," Ada almost dismisses as mere "philosophical amusement," perhaps because she is on guard to have the engine perceived as of "great practical utility" and perhaps also because of the Newtonian admonition against advancing unconfirmed hypotheses.

"NOTE G"

The most forbidding note in some sections for the general reader, "Note G" also contains the most frequently quoted observation, which begins: "It is desirable to guard against the possibility of exaggerated ideas that might arise as to the power of the Analytical Engine." Ada recognized the dangers of discovery: first, the disposition to *"overrate* what we find to be already interesting or remarkable"; and then, in compensation, a willingness to *"undervalue* the true state of the case." This opening paragraph, which she revised many times, constitutes a natural preamble to the often-quoted paragraph that follows,

called by some "lady Lovelace's Objection," though a more
familiar reference might be "GIGO," "garbage in, garbage out":

The Analytical Engine has no pretensions whatever to *originate*
anything. It can do whatever we *know how to order it* to perform. It
can *follow* analysis; but it has no power of *anticipating* any analytical relations or truths. Its province is to assist us in making
available what we are already acquainted with.

Prescient or trivial? Critics cannot decide, but the answer may
require a different description, such as "informed dreaming."
Of course, Ada could not see the implications of her comments
for the age of artificial intelligence, but the passage suggests that
she may have anticipated the semantic debates that would arise
over the meaning of words *creative* and *brain*. The Analytical
Engine will probably exert an "*indirect* and reciprocal influence
on science itself," she predicts, as logical relations and the
nature of subjects set for the engine will be necessarily re-
arranged and thus reexamined. It is a theme to which she kept
returning.

"Note G" goes on to sum up the "chief elements with which
the engine works," including integration and differentiation,
and it concludes with a detailed account of how the engine
could compute the numbers of Bernoulli, "a rather complicated
example of its powers." It is this section of the "Notes" that
Bowden singled out as evidence that Ada Lovelace was "a
mathematician of great competence" with interests in many
branches of the discipline.[15] It is also this section that proves, in a
way, that Ada was indeed "the world's first computer programmer": in showing how the Analytical Engine could compute the
Bernoulli numbers, Ada was in effect writing a complex "program." Named by Euler for Jakob Bernoulli (1654–1705), one of
the pioneers of probability theory (and coiner of the term
integral), and first described in a posthumous publication, *Ars
Conjectandi* (1713), the Bernoulli numbers attracted, among others, Peacock (in 1820) and Plana. Ada was proud of her handling
of the sequence and wrote to Babbage that the diagram was
done in "a beautiful manner," though there were some errors
she would correct. In generating the Bernoulli numbers, Ada
was showing how "an implicit function may be worked out by
the engine, without having been worked out by human head &

hands first"[16]—an illustration that would demonstrate the engine's ability to increase its own power, since the Bernoulli numbers constitute a sequence that increases with rapidity. Unlike explicit functions whose expansion formula might be guessed at, the Bernoulli numbers, so irregular to look at, were an apt choice to "program" onto a machine. Bernoulli himself had claimed that by using the numbers, he found the sum of the tenth powers of the first thousand integers in half a quarter of an hour.

Ada's work on the Bernoulli numbers validates her role as expositor, although some critics question her originality. Brian Randall, in *(The Origin of Digital Computers)*[17] claims that the "program" was first drawn up by Babbage, with Ada assisting. Drafts of "Note G" did go back and forth often between Babbage and Ada, but it was Ada who seemed to be in command; it was even she who "detected a grave mistake" which Babbage had made.[18] In *Passages*, Babbage said that the selection of illustrations, or programs, for the "Notes" was entirely Lady Lovelace's, as was the algebraic working out of the different problems. She "entered fully into almost all the very difficult and abstract questions," he wrote, so much so that she should have expanded the "Notes" and brought them out under her own name, since she was so "intimately acquainted" with all the concepts.

Ada had worked "doggedly" (one of her favorite words) on "Note G," on both text and diagram, as she wrote Babbage and as letters between them confirm. The Bernoulli numbers table, the one her husband had helped her ink over, particularly pleased her, and he, she reported, was "quite enchanted" with its *"beauty & symmetry."* Lord Lovelace was indeed delighted with his wife's accomplishment. Although she had not been attending to many household functions, her mathematical activities were important to her, he saw, and to his own hopes of advancing in society. It must have puzzled him, therefore, before it began to sadden him, that after the "Notes" were published, Ada said she still needed to get away to work. The problem was, there was nothing specific to work on. Was it at about this time that she took to gambling and to seeing a bit more of Andrew Crosse's son, John?

[CHAPTER 6]

Yearnings
and Defeat

Despite attempts to sound casual, Ada was delighted to be published in *Taylor's Scientific Memoirs*, a "very valuable periodical."[1] She clucked over the proofs with fastidious concern. In letters to Richard Taylor, highly formal, nervously fussy communications, she refers to herself in the third person and reminds Taylor, one of the most important science editors in England, to ensure that "*every particular care & accuracy* be observed." She was aware that the nature and extent of her "Notes" placed them outside Taylor's usual plan, and she was apologetic for having caused delays, adding that she could by no means flatter herself that the "Notes" "possessed any *intrinsic* value sufficient to justify an *exception* being made in their favor.[2] But in truth she really hoped they would be perceived as significant.

It is reasonable to suppose that the leading men of science of the day purchased copies of *Taylor's Scientific Memoirs*, but since translations were not reviewed and admiring statements could be expected from friends and certain acquaintances, it is difficult to assess just what Ada's contemporaries thought of her effort. Like Byron, Ada could affect indifference, but letters to family and close friends show she valued praise. Early in 1843, during the composition of "Note A," Babbage wondered if Prince Albert might be sent a copy of the full annotation, a suggestion Ada dismissed at the time as not expedient. But this may have been caution talking more than propriety, intellectual nervousness rather than a restraining sense of decorum. In August, shortly before the "Notes" were published, Lady Byron mentioned some reported curiosity about Ada's work. The "Notes" were no secret, Ada responded, but they were "not worth either making a mystery of or particularly proclaiming." She thought it "very natural that many persons must be acquainted with the fact that I have been writing something or other."[3] Indeed.

After publication, she ordered 250 offprints. Michael Faraday, who received a copy, complimented her on her high objects, views, determination, hopes, mind, and powers, "now made fully manifest to others." He praised her "elasticity" of intellect, she wrote Lady Byron, and then, in a burst of hyperbole, she declared that Faraday regarded her as "the rising star of science." "You drive me to desperation by your invitations,"[4] he had written, she eager to have him come by, he unable to comply. Was Ada thinking of Faraday as a new "Man" in her intellectual life? Ironically, Faraday cautioned Ada not to expect too much help from him, for "nature is against you." He meant that he was getting on while she had the advantages of youth. Faraday died in 1867, Ada in 1852.

Even before the "Notes" were published, Ada could not disguise her enthusiasm. "Oh dear! How merciless [William] carried off my proofs & revises to some of his friends who came here; despite my remonstrances as to their blotted and unintelligible State!—" After publication, admiration came from the various mentors. Ada had sent Mrs. Somerville a copy, which was read "with great interest." Mrs. Somerville praised the "proficiency you have made in the highest branches of mathematics & the clearness with which you have illustrated a very difficult subject. . . ."[5] Mr. Babbage "must be truly gratified in having such a commentator." Mrs. Somerville reserved her most moving comments, however, for expressions of personal concern. Like De Morgan, Mrs. Somerville was worried, having heard that Ada was looking thin and was far from strong, and like De Morgan she would attribute much of that enervation to Ada's pursuit of mathematics. By the fall of 1843, Ada was taking sedatives and stimulants for recurring neurological and intestinal disorders.

De Morgan, convinced that a stronger Ada would have produced better work, nonetheless wrote that the "Notes" were admirable. Delighted, Ada sent Babbage a copy of De Morgan's *"kind* and *approving* letter," adding, somewhat disingenuously, "Imagine! I never expected that *he* would view my crude young composition so favourably."[6] Probably it would have been Babbage's regard that would most impress her, but that would not be given publicly for twenty years, and then just once, in *Passages*. Wary about making statements about his beloved engines because plans were not yet in the form he wanted them, and growing increasingly depressed and bitter, Babbage in 1844 must have perceived that Ada's energies were not as concentrated as his own on his great machine. He may also have perceived that her energies were not exactly concentrated on mathematics, either. But he was sincere in his praise: ". . . the more I read your notes the more surprised I am at them and regret not having earlier explored so rich a vein of the noblest metal." He spoke of the "Notes" as an "original paper." To have described the successive improvements of the Analytical Engine would have required many volumes, and even the "most enlightened" did not understand.

An oblique comment by Elizabeth Barrett Browning suggests the extent of Babbage's quarrels and difficulties, but also of his stubbornness. "Do you know Tennyson?" she wrote to Robert Browning in 1845. "That is with a face to face knowledge? I have great admiration for him. . . . That such a poet sh'd submit blindly to the suggestion of his critics is much as if Babbage were to take my opinion and undo his calculating machine by it."[7] How deeply Babbage was involved with his grievances over the engine may be divined from the disagreement he had with Ada shortly before publication of the "Notes." He had wanted to broaden her work to include another version of his rejection by the government. Ada, sensing perhaps that her annotation would be put in shadow, called him *"selfish & intemperate"* and declared she did not want to be the *"organ"* of his arguments. It was a tense time: he, not in the best of health, had temporarily misplaced some sections; she, in intermittent pain, and in constant frustration over printer's errors, was trying to sort out and clarify minute details. A month later they were friends, and the "Notes" came out. But so did another Babbage explanation, one month after that, in Taylor's *Philosophical Magazine:* a "Statement of the Circumstances Attending the Invention and Construction of Mr. Babbage's Engines."[8] Babbage referred to the piece as an "addition" to the memoir of M. Menabrea, the "distinguished Italian Geometer" who drew "an excellent account of the Engine." There was no mention of Ada Lovelace. It would remain for C. R. Weld, in his *History of the Royal Society* (1848), to give praise to "the English Translation [of Menabrea] with copious original notes made by a lady of distinguished rank and talent."[9] Only in Weld's footnote was there acknowledgment: "I am authorized by Lord Lovelace to say that the translator is Lady Lovelace." By that time, however, though statements of Ada's mathematical intention would continue, there was no more extensive talk between Ada and Babbage about the Analytical Engine.

In August of 1843, as though anticipating a postpartum depression, Ada had written Babbage shortly before the "child" was delivered that she was thinking of continuing their relationship beyond the "Notes." It was an audacious statement, really an inquiry, and part of a long letter which contained, among other things, expressions of anger over his editing and suggestion of delay. Did he want her to remain in his service? If so, there were conditions—a first, second, and third followed—rules for allowing the Lovelaces to manage the business and politics of getting the engine constructed. Babbage would have to agree to let them make the decisions. She spoke, she said, for both Lovelace and herself, but it is the rebellious and nervous acolyte who comes through. Of course, if Babbage is not interested in having her assist him any more, he has "*first* choice" of refusal. She owes him that. Meanwhile, writing to Lord Lovelace, Ada concluded, "I had better continue to be simply the High Priestess of Babbage's Engine, and serve my apprenticeship faithfully therein, before I fancy myself worthy to approach a step higher towards being the High Priestess of God Almighty Himself."[10] Lovelace was put on notice. And what if further work with Babbage could not be arranged? She would not be idle. She would "throw my energies, my time & pen into the service of some other department of truth & science." She had in July written to Babbage about doing a "long" review of "Ohm's litle work" in the autumn (probably the pamphlet "On galvanic series, mathematically determined," for the *Philosophical Magazine*), though for this endeavor she would want to rely on him more: "I don't yet know enough to be sure always of the *solidity* or *appositeness* of my findings."[11]

To her mother, around the same time, she had written that the "Notes" would be *"followed up."* There were "various subjects" on which she would publish. Various channels, some "very attractive," was the way she expressed it to Babbage. She would develop her "scientific and literary powers" in any case. One year later, in 1844, she would be writing Greig about putting her horrific experience with opium and wine to scientific advantage: she was contemplating the collection of *"cerebral* phenomena such that I can put them into mathematical equations; in short a law or laws for the mutual action of the molecules of *brain;* (equivalent to the law of *gravitation* for the planetary and *sidereal* world)." She was already proceeding on a track "quite peculiar & my own," and someday, she wrote to Lord Lovelace during this same period, she hoped to bequeath to the world a *"Calculus of the Nervous System."* She looked to learn how to be a "most skilful practical manipulator in experimental tests," with materials having to deal with the brain, blood, and nerves of animals.[12] A few months earlier, De Morgan had written somewhat defensively to Lady Byron about the constancy of Ada's devotion to mathematics. Would what Ada called her *"external unextinguishable* flame of love" for mathematics really be seductive enough for a lifetime? There is easily seen to be "the desire of distinction in Lady L's character," De Morgan conceded, "but the mathematical turn is one which opportunity must have made her take independently of that."[13] If Lady Byron and Lord Lovelace concluded that "desire of distinction" was Ada's main motive, and "science one of the many paths which might be chosen to obtain it," they would be mistaken. Obviously, Lady Byron and Lord Lovelace thought they saw something else in spite of Ada's continuing declarations of mathematical devotion.

In August, when the "Notes" were completed, Ada was writing that despite all the "trouble & *interminable* labour of having to revise the printing of *mathematical* formulae," there would be "many hundreds & thousands of such formulae" that would "come forth from my pen, in one way or another." Her *"first-born,"* she declared, was characterized chiefly by *"strong sense;* a union of the most minute & laborious accuracy . . . he will make an excellent *head* (I hope) of a *large* family of brothers & sisters; . . ." In fact, Ada continued, William was eager for her to do more work, because they believed it was "desirous" that she give an impression of being "completely tied down & committed to the scientific & literary line." Such activity would place her in a much *"juster and truer* position & light" and place William *"in a far more agreeable position in this country."*

Apparently she was ready to do more translations. By the 1840s German had come to be as important a language as French in the scientific community, since mathematical hegemony was shifting to Berlin and Göttingen, and to academies specializing in theoretical physics and number theory. German scientists were also being courted by the British Association. It is possible that Ada was thinking of translating Mitscherlich's "Chemical Reactions Produced by Bodies Which Act Only by Contact" (1841). Mitscherlich held the chief chair in chemistry at Berlin and was a specialist in crystallography, a field in which Ada had expressed interest to Andrew Crosse.[14] Indeed, Andrew Crosse's son John had been particularly encouraging. It was his idea, and Wheatstone's, she wrote Lovelace, that she "study with a view to writing scientific treatises in German." "John Crosse says that in Germany books of *dry science sell* even better than light works. . . . I believe that many of *my* subjects would be read to an extent in *that* country, which they never would here (besides paying well) . . . I know very *nearly* enough of the language." Young Crosse's presence nearby would be helpful, she added. "I can get from him & by means of him, what I could from no one else."[15] It would prove to be an ironically unfortunate prediction.

John Crosse was not Ada's first dalliance, but he was the most dangerous. By 1843, the year the "Notes" were published, some of Ada's mild flirtations were becoming known. Babbage was privy to Ada's amusements with one Frederick Knight, but so, apparently, were the newspapers: "The resemblance of Lady

Lovelace to her renowned father, beyond some parental like-
ness, has as yet been confined to a certain amount of eccentricity." By 1843 she didn't seem to care that she was frequently
seen in Knight's company, suiting her "dress" to his "address."[16]
In the same year, Lady Byron hired, and Lady Lovelace fired,
Dr. William Benjamin Carpenter as tutor to the Lovelace children. Carpenter was exactly Ada's age, and Ada had begun to
speak with him privately about her despondency and restlessness, about her glasses of claret at dinner and her glasses of
claret in place of dinner. In 1849, Carpenter would win a prize
for "On the Use and Abuse of Alcoholic Liquids." He would win
no awards for his behavior with the Lovelaces. Smitten with
Ada, flattered, naïvely indiscreet, he took her flirtation for more
than its worth and wrote to Lord Lovelace about certain verbal
intimacies, private conversations he had had with Lady Lovelace at her urging, expectations never realized but which she
had aroused by her manner. At what point the notorious John
Crosse became a confidant is not clear, nor is the full extent of
his personal and professional involvement with Ada. But the
fact remains that he would prove threatening enough to cause
Lord Lovelace, Greig, Babbage, and Lady Byron to reclaim and
destroy the bulk of an extensive correspondence between
Crosse and Ada, estimated by Lovelace to have been 108 letters.

What Ada seemed to need more than some*thing* scientific was
some*one* scientific. With the "Notes" published and Babbage
otherwise absorbed, Ada may have had second thoughts about
the Prince Consort. The year was 1844 and Ada was ready to
announce herself a *"woman"* of science. She had heard through
friends that Prince Albert, a *"very* clever young man" (though
not brilliant), was desirous of being "at the head of a *scientific*
circle in England."[17] He was twenty-five at the time, Ada
twenty-nine. Wheatstone had suggested that the prince could
be properly advised only "by some *woman* [who] can put him in
the right way, & open the *door* to him towards all he desires; &
that a *woman* can say that which any *man* would get into a scrape
by doing," she wrote Lovelace that year. Further, Wheatstone
had suggested she not do anything immediate but acquire
instead some "standing" in the next few years. Then the prince
would take notice and speak to her "about *science*," about what

he might support and where he might best lend his influence. Ada was full of high spirits. The result of her advising the prince, she continued, would be her doing for science "an *inestimable benefit.*" It did not occur to her that the proper woman to advise the prince might be someone else—Mrs. Somerville, perhaps—who already had record and reputation. Six years later Lovelace would write Lady Byron that he wished Queen Victoria "saw more or rather something of Ada—the gt Ly would be all the better for the genuineness of the truths she might have to hear—but it seems as if the links of the court circle are accidentally formed & yet firmly closed around casual admissions from without. . . ."[18] Some years earlier, Babbage had probably concluded as much about rank over merit.

Despite intentions, the "woman" of science found herself after 1843 without a project to capture her imagination. Restlessness was setting in, and from 1844 on there were new medical disorders—back pains, swellings, cold spells, trouble with kidneys and, two years later, gastritis and asthma. She could joke about her indispositions, apologizing on one occasion to John Murray, at whose dinner party during the 1846 season she had collapsed. "*Spasms of the heart,*" she conjectured, which she had for twenty years, but "It might be worse; some organic disease, cancer, unsound lungs—God knows what, for unhappy diseases abound."[19] She hoped that "*desirable oscillation*" would soon come round, as indeed it did. There were respites, periods of good health, the last as late as 1851, when she went hiking in the Lake District. She came to love journeys to the north, particularly after 1850, because they were associated with Nottinghamshire, her father's country. It was only then, two years before she died, that Ada Lovelace finally saw Newstead Abbey, the Byron ancestral home, and Hucknall Torkard, where her father lay buried. Depression, the first reaction, gave way to morbid attraction, and then to a great feeling of attachment. "Altogether it is an *epoch* in my life, my visit there. I have lost my *monumental & desolate* feeling respecting it.—It seemed like descending into the *grave,* but I have had a *resurrection.* I do love the venerable old place & all my *wicked forefathers!*[20] The tradition, she might have added, was being continued. Byron's dying words, it was reported, had been about her: "Oh, my poor dear child!—my dear Ada! my God, could I but have seen her! Give her my blessing—"[21] She needed it. Long before she began to be destroyed by the *"monster"* that would devour her system, as she would later describe the cancer she knew was killing her, she had begun a descent into a hell all her own.

She had been betting, and seeing an extensive and unhealthy amount of John Crosse. There had been debts as early as 1848, when, unknown to Lovelace, Greig had had to write to a bank on Ada's behalf. By Derby Day, May 21, 1851, Ada had reached the end of a frazzled line. She owed £2,000, a fact that does not argue well for allegations that she and Babbage had doped out a means of winning at the races. The direct evidence that survives is scanty—a few racing receipts, some letters to Babbage asking that he settle accounts on her behalf. But there is indirect evidence enough, as well as Lord Lovelace's journal, begun the months before she died.

She liked horses. She liked men of science. She liked the idea of living dangerously and, increasingly, seemed to act on it. She seems not to have known or cared that John Crosse was married and had children, that he was a gambling man. He wrote her when she was away from home and not using the Lovelace name. He had in his possession a private note that Lovelace had sent to Ada, authorizing a minor bet—a kind of last hurrah, perhaps, to win her over on a promise of withdrawal. Babbage and Greig were disturbed and saddened. On her deathbed she asked to see two people. Babbage was one of them; Lady Byron prevented it. The other was John Crosse. The "extortioner," Lovelace called him. The "Enchantress of Numbers" had done more than flirted around. She had lent Crosse money, pawned the family jewels, given her heart away.

Upon her death, the usually restrained Lovelace would finally acknowledge the depth of her entanglements. "For the past week I have been a prey to the utmost wretchedness of mind— Every cherished conviction of my married life has been unsettled." He wrote of "evil," the full extent of which even Lady Byron would never know, of the "torture" that Ada's misconduct had inflicted on him, of "grave crimes." By now, Lady Byron had turned her enmity upon her once adored son-in-law. It was he (and Babbage too, of course) who was responsible for

Ada's degeneration and for a coolness that had crept into the relationship between mother and child. But Lovelace suspected the real reason for the estrangement, Ada's realization—acknowledged, perhaps, on that visit to Newstead Abbey—of her mother's managed account of Lord Byron. "I will not now mention the primary and indelible cause of the alienation between you and her [sic] it was expressly alluded to by her since May last—and it had occurred long before my acquaintance with your family."[22]

By January 1852, acute agony from uterine cancer had begun—prolonged, excruciating pain, unrelieved by drugs or mesmerism. Incredibly, however, as Lovelace observed, Ada's mental energy seemed to be unflagging:

> Her mind was invigorated by the society of the intellectual men whom she entertained as guests. . . . She mastered the mathematical side of a question in all its minuteness. . . . Her power of generalisation was indeed most remarkable, coupled as it was with that of minute & intricate analysis. Babbage was a constant intellectual companion & she ever found in him a match for her powerful understanding, their constant philosophical discussions begetting only an increased esteem & mutual liking.[23]

Despite descending spirals into nets woven by the gods and by her own blind passions, the bird could still fly high on fantasies of mathematical grandeur. In October of 1851, the year before she died, there had been a letter from Lady Byron about political matters. Ada had replied that she wished she could give the despots a shove, as she would then feel she had not lived in vain. But it was not just politics she was talking about. The letter continued with underlining and double underlining to describe an extravagant imagining:

> I think . . . when you see certain productions, you will not even despair of my being *in time* an *Autocrat*, in my own way, before whose *marshalled regiments* some of the iron rulers of the earth may even have to give way. But of *what materials* my *regiments* are to consist, I do not at present divulge.
>
>   I have however the hope that they will be most *harmoniously* disciplined troops;—consisting of vast *numbers*, & marching in irresistible power to the sound of *Music*. Is not this very mysterious? Certainly *my* troops must consist of *numbers* or they can have

no existence at all, & would cease to be the particular sort of troops in question.—But then, *what* are these *Numbers?* There is a riddle—[24]

It was never explained.

Ada Lovelace was a small star whose shining had mattered to Charles Babbage and then burned out. When she died, the *London Times* on November 27, 1852, referred to the death of "Augusta Ada, wife of William Earl of Lovelace and only daughter of George Gordon Noel Lord Byron, after a long and painful illness borne with utmost patience and fortitude. She left behind two sons and a daughter." Nothing was said about her work. Five years later, in tribute to her, Babbage sent her elder son, Ockham, a "Table of Logs" run off by inventors of a Swedish difference engine, modeled on his own, and these words: "In the memoir of Mr. Menabrea and still more in the excellent Notes appended by your mother you will find the only comprehensive view of the powers of the Anal. Eng. which the mathematicians of the world have yet expressed."[25] The late Countess Lovelace had the "highest claim" on his "respect" among the departed friends who had stood by him.

She need not have done more. Her place in mathematical science, though small, is legitimate. "Still more" than Menabrea, Babbage had written, Ada in her "excellent Notes" gave the "only comprehensive view" of the "powers" of the Analytical Engine. Did he mean it?[26] It would seem so. Ada Lovelace concentrated on the "powers" of the Analytical Engine by explaining its mathematical principles and writing a program for it to illustrate that power. Hers was not the only exposition, but it was the first extensive explanation and illustration of how such a machine could receive, store, manipulate, and print out data given numerically, literally, and symbolically. And it was, until recently, "the only clear statement we possess of Babbage's views on the scope of his engines" as Hyman points out.[27] Without knowing that such functions would become the soul of the modern-day computer, Ada noted the engine's ability to do repetitions and loops and to change course in midstream. Her speculations about its future power were the inevitable dilations of one who saw herself a "prophetess" as much as an expositor. That she expressed such hopes, made such claims, is of no consequence in the history of science. But her story is. To have studied mathematics then to the degree she did was unusual; to have been curious about what would become a century later one of the most significant developments in mathematics is important enough to be commemorated with a programming language. To pay Lady Lovelace honor is to acknowledge her activity, not to inflate her achievement. In fact, her influence in the history of computing is finally no more than that of Babbage, who, for all his genius, died unsung.

A curiosity in literature, an anomaly in the history of science, a mystery, still, because evidence is incomplete, Ada Lovelace was indeed, even if by accident, the world's first computer programmer. The program she devised for Babbage's Analytical Engine was the first complex set of instructions written for a mechanism that would receive data (input), perform complicated operations (calculate), and conclude in results (output, including print). The generated sequence of Bernoulli numbers was clearly an advance on the comparatively simple linear algorithms that existed for calculating machines or for weaving looms—instructions that said, in effect, first do this, then that; sequences that went one way only and that, for all their ingeniousness, were limited. The fact is, however, that the Analytical Engine was never built, and Ada's display of the Bernoulli numbers in "Note G", while it shows off the potential of the engine, is too specialized for general readers and of historical interest only to mathematicians. The claim of "world's first computer programmer," therefore, while valid, is not necessarily significant. But it is instructive. Ada Lovelace generally understood the basic principles of Babbage's Analytical Engine. More important, however, if not *as* history but *in* history, was her intuition about what such a machine *might* do. Even if the insights seem the incidental thoughts of a dilettante, they grew out of impassioned and reflective thinking about the Analytical Engine and about the kind of mathematical problems it might be set to solve.

What is noticeable about some sections of the "Notes," what

is wonderful, is their fancy and imagination, poetic qualities which show essentially not mathematical expertise (however debatable) but the kind of creative play that often leads to mathematical invention. For Ada, the exercise of a speculating fancy gave pleasure and release. Referring to Babbage's allusion to her "fairy" similes, she writes back, ' "Why does my friend prefer *imaginary* roots for our friendship?'—Just because she happens to have some of that very imagination which *you* would deny her to possess; & therefore she enjoys a little *play* & *scope* for it now & then. Besides this, I deny the *Fairyism* to be entirely *imaginary*."[28]

Ada Lovelace was the world's first extensive expositor of a computing machine. She was also a fascinating woman, interesting as much for her motives as for her work, illustrating as she does the theme of creative energy in collision with suppressed desire. "Fancy me in times of social & political trouble, (had *worldly* power, rule & ambition been my line, which it now [1843] never could be)," she mused to Babbage. *"Her"* kingdom, however, would not be a *"temporal"* one. Then, with a dramatic sweep undercut with irony, the ultimate Byron combination, she continued—it would be "well for the world" that she did not take up sword, poison, intrigue in place of "x,y,&z."[29]

As she lay dying, Lovelace recorded in his journal he recalled for her "how often in our rambles among the hills I had observed her eyes gazing wistfully into space as though ready to float off into the future. She smiled assent with a melancholy pleasure."

Cancer was not her fate; character was.

Appendix 1: Ada
in Byron's Poetry

From "Fare thee well" (a poem of 15 quatrains, written March 17, 1816)[1]

stanza six

And when thou wouldst solace gather,
When our child's first accents flow,
Wilt thou teach her to say 'Father!'
Though his care she must forego?

From *Childe Harold's Pilgrimage*, Canto III[2]

stanza i

Is thy face like thy mother's, my fair child!
ADA! sole daughter of my house and heart?
When last I saw thy young blue eyes they smiled,
And when we parted—not as now we part,
But with a hope.—
                Awaking with a start.
The waters heave around me; and on high
The winds lift up their voices; I depart,
Whither I know not; but the hour's gone by,
When Albion's lessening shores could grieve
                or glad mine eye.

stanza cxv

My daughter! with thy name this song begun!
My daughter! with thy name thus much shall end!—
I see thee not—I hear thee not—but none
Can be so wrapt in thee; Thou art the Friend
To whom the shadows of far years extend;

Albeit my brow thou never should'st behold,
My voice shall with thy future visions blend,
And reach into thy heart,—when mine is cold,—
A token and a tone, even from thy father's mould.

stanza cxviii

The child of Love! though born in bitterness,
And nurtured in Convulsion! Of thy sire
These were the elements,—and thine no less.
As yet such are around thee,—but thy fire
Shall be more tempered, and thy hope far higher!
Sweet be thy cradled slumbers! O'er the sea
And from the mountains where I now respire,
Fain would I waft such blessing upon thee,
As—with a sigh—I deem thou might'st have
                    been to me!

A poem by Ada

"The Rainbow" by "A.A.L.", n.d.

Bow down in hope, in thanks, all ye who mourn;—
    Whene'er that peerless arch of radiant hues
Surpassing earthly tints,—the storm subdues!
    Of nature's strife and tears 'tis heaven-born,
To soothe the sad, the sinning and forlorn;
        A lovely loving token to infuse
        The hope, the faith, that pow'r divine endues
With latent good the woes by which we're torn—
'Tis like a sweet repentence of the skies,
    To beckon all by sense of sin opprest,
Revealing harmony from tears and sighs!
A pledge,—that deep implanted in the breast
A hidden light may burn that never dies,
But burst thro' storms in purest hues earnest!

Appendix 2: The Victorian
Medical World

In July, four months before Ada died, Lord Lovelace wrote Greig that he quite feared asking for any definite opinion of the doctor who was treating her.[1] Months earlier, however, Ada herself had faced the truth: "I understand the uterus is *destroyed* as to all vital functions." Locock had diagnosed the disease as cancer but called it "treatable." What this meant is not clear, considering the deep ulceration of the neck and mouth of the womb he reported and the absence of any treatment to arrest developent or reduce pain.

A lecturer at St. Bartholomew's Hospital, a physician at Westminster Lying-In, a member of the Royal College of Physicians, and, in 1840, first physician to the queen, Locock (1799–1875) reportedly had the "best practice in London as an accoucheur." The *DNB* notes that he was also a man of skill and a good storyteller but that he had "little scientific power" or imagination. His social position and medical limitations, typical of the time, illustrate the relatively poor state of medicine in the first half of the nineteenth century. Indeed, medicine was the least of the academic concerns at British Association meetings. In 1838, for example, of thirty-one members nominated to the steering committee of the BAAS, only one represented the medical sciences, and he was hardly prominent. Excluded from research grants and given little attention from the executive board of the BAAS, the medical section went into "rapid decline" as leading physicians, surgeons, and physiologists stopped submitting papers.[2]

Regardless, nothing could have helped Ada Lovelace in 1852. What was known about uterine cancer was by way of autopsy.

Treatment, so-called, consisted mainly of prescribing various anodynes, but even the morphia administered to Ada in her final months obviously did not bring her relief. Surgery would have been out of the question. Operations were occasionally performed, but it was the official and respected position of physicians that they should be avoided. Dr. Robert Lee, whose special interest was the pathology of women's diseases, wrote in the *Cyclopaedia of Practical Medicine* (1854) that "it must appear unnecessary to pass sentence of condemnation upon the practice of removing the uterus, either wholly or partially, when affected with malignant disease. The operation appears to us equally cruel and unscientific."[3]

What seems extraordinary is just how much was known about uterine cancer in the mid-nineteenth century. The *Cyclopaedia*, for example, gives over seven pages of double-column description to the disease, and the period coincides with early uses of anesthesia, though it was used experimentally and against a good deal of medical and moral opposition. Coincidentally, on the very day Ada died, the *London Times* supplement carried an advertisement announcing the opening of the first cancer hospital in London "for the reception of in-door patients." Persons afflicted with the malady would be admitted by personal application, it continued, but it seems safe to say that the institution was probably no more than a lock-up facility for the indigent. Doctors such as Locock or Lee would have "consulted" as attending physicians, but they would not legally have performed surgery or administered drugs, there or anywhere.

The medical world of Ada Lovelace's day was divided into three parts, though surgeons and apothecaries merged to some extent through cross-licensing. The separations reflected class distinctions, still in evidence today, and accounted for the often wide disparity between diagnosis and treatment. Anatomy and physiology, the specialties of Henry Acland (himself a physician and later a professor of medicine at Oxford), were still too new and poorly integrated into medical education then to count for much. Locock, a member of the Profession of Physic, thus belonged to the most prestigious medical group, the Royal College of Physicians in London, but it constituted only five percent of the total medical profession, primarily those who boasted a classical Oxbridge education rather than practical training or apothecary lore. Physicians taught anatomy but did not perform operations; they administered drugs but knew little of their composition or multiple effects.[4] Apothecaries, on the other hand, were skilled craftsmen whose field of operation, so to speak, was only the external body. No wonder that as Lady Lovelace entered a prolonged siege of cancer pain, all manner of alleged pain suppressents were tried—leeches, wine, opium, mesmerism. The same front page announcing the opening of the London Cancer Hospital also carried an advertisement for the reestablishment of the London Phrenological Society. Lady Byron would have been pleased.

Appendix 3: Ada in Twentieth-Century Literature

The Babbage scholar Garry Tee, who has read Lewis Carroll's "profound masterpiece" *The Hunting of the Snark* (1876) in the annotated edition by Martin Gardner, wonders if the *Snark* might not contain allusions to Babbage and Ada Lovelace.[1] Like Babbage, Charles Lutwidge Dodgson, professor of mathematics at Christ Church, Oxford, was fond of puzzles, puns, and games. Might the Beaver who makes lace be Lady Lovelace; the Butcher, who sharpens his axe, Babbage, who published a paper in 1836 on cutting tools? The Beaver and the Butcher become good friends. Holiday's illustrations, Tee suggests, may be particularly telling. The Butcher gives arithmetic lessons to the Beaver but is distracted by organ-grinders and a wind band, a motley crew depicted as demons and pigs. The lizard picking the pocket of the Butcher has a paper labelled "Income Tax," suggesting Babbage's 1848 pamphlet on the subject. The Baker's advice to the Beaver is "to insure its life in some office of note," which might be an allusion to Ada's annotations. But a reader might also wonder if the Bellman might not stand for Babbage as well, since the Difference Engine had an ingenious design for a bell that would ring to adjust data cards.

Asked about Babbage-Lovelace allusions, Martin Gardner replies that such suggestions strain credulity: "I checked the indices of all the books I have on Carroll—including his diaries, collected letters, etc.—and find no references to Babbage or Ada. So far as I know, he never mentioned either of them." Gardner prefers to play with an existential interpretation of

Snark—that "impossible voyage of an improbable crew to find an inconceivable creature." He fastens on different details, noting that the poem is an "Agony in Eight Fyttes," a "fit" being an archaic word for a division of a poem or song.[2] Coincidentally, the *Oxford English Dictionary on Historical Principles* cites Byron in illustration: "Here is one fytte of [Childe] Harold's pilgrimage" (canto one, stanza xciii). Another coincidence is more striking. Lewis Carroll antedates Ada in contributing to military names. In the 1960s, the U.S. Air Force had a missile called the Snark.

Denying Lovelace implications in the *Snark*, Gardner suggests that they may be found in Vladimir Nabokov's *Ada or Ardor: A Family Chronicle* (1969), an elaborate parodic love story and disquisition on time, which also contains a punning reference to Lewis Carroll:

> "Playing croquet with you," said Van, "should be rather like using flamingoes and hedgehogs."
> "Our reading lists do not match," replied Ada [Veen] "That *Palace in Wonderland* was to me the kind of book everybody so often promised me I would adore, that I developed an insurmountable prejudice against it."[3]

Is Ada Veen conceived, in part, on the model of Ada Lovelace? Byron's name is invoked in the Nabokov novel. Both Adas are intelligent, witty, bold, and direct-talking aristocrats. Ada Veen, like Ada Lovelace, has a deep and abiding love for science and music. Ada Veen would be a biologist, she tells her cousin and lover Van Veen, a Byron-like character who may also be her half-brother. Her "passion" for entymology is "great," but not, she admits, all-consuming. Ada Veen, like Ada Lovelace, can be flirtatious and seductive, but Ada Veen is supremely aware of her tragic flaws and consistently ironic in her response to the limits space and time place on her energies. Born in 1872, Ada Veen is a good half-century older than her possible real-life counterpart and much richer, philosophically.

Ironically, the most explicit reference to Ada Lovelace in modern literature is a play about her based on a fiction. In *Childe Byron*, playwright Romulus Linney gives Ada a chance to question the father she never knew. "I was your creation," she tells him imperiously, after summoning him forth in a drug-induced fantasy; "now you are mine."[4] Linney's 1975 play is a literate, witty, clever exploration of a nonexistent relationship, a dramatic series of vignettes about Byron, Lady Byron, and Ada, with the same actress playing in both female roles. Ada's cool will meets Byron's passion when she challenges him to relive his life and explain his actions. Lines from poems are used in the disclosures. A small-scale model of the Difference Engine sits onstage. Byron's pistols are on the mantel. Linney's Ada speaks as Ada Lovelace wrote; he has caught her bold, crisp manner. It was, in fact, he writes, her prose style that captivated him, and that gave him the idea to make her central in a drama he had been commissioned to write about Byron. *Childe Byron* is a touching portrayal and an ironic one. After all, it is Ada's imagination that directs the dialogue and a twentieth-century point of view that controls the Victorian one. Through her fantasy, Ada finally gets to possess the father she never knew and to resolve her ambivalence, first by forgiving Byron, and then by realizing how much she resembles him.

Appendix 4: The Ada Programming Language

Although Babbage had a mountain peak named after him in his lifetime, the honor was in New South Wales and nothing special. And even considering other Babbage additions to the landscape—a river, an island and, in 1862, a lunar crater[1]—Ada Lovelace eclipsed Charles Babbage in posterity: she was given a language.[2]

On December 12, 1980, 165 years to the day after Ada Byron's birth, the Office of the Principal Deputy Under Secretary of Defense for Research and Engineering announced the birth of the Ada Joint Program Office (AJPO) to "provide centralized management of the total Department of Defense effort to implement, introduce and provide lifecycle support for Ada. . . ."[3] An Ada language was now endorsed as a large-scale engineering project for embedded computer systems applications.

On February 17, 1983, the American National Standards Institute (ANSI) approved Ada as a national all-purpose standard, in document number MIL-STD-1815—the number in honor of Ada's birth year. Approval is pending for international recognition, and discussion continues about standardizing the Ada "programming environment." Babbage's reason for developing an Analytical Engine had been to meet the need for standardized fast, efficient, and error-free computations, which was also the primary motive of the Department of Defense in seeking a new programming language. The hallmark of Ada is said to be its capacity for modular design and for specifying data types (integer, character, string, array, etc.) that reduce the risk of error and debugging time.[4] Coincidentally, the Ada language is designed for "fourth-generation" technology, and it was a fourth-generation Ada Lovelace descendant, the late Lord Lytton (d. 1985), who gave his approval to the department for use of Ada's name.[5]

The language was conceived in 1974, 140 years after Lady Lovelace first saw plans for the Analytical Engine. By 1834, the British government had invested a small fortune in Babbage's machines. By 1974, the United States military had spent more than $25 billion on software and hardware design, not to mention costs for maintenance and production.

Given Lady Lovelace's stated desire to put mathematics to useful purpose, she might not have objected to having a "higher order" language named after her, especially one that would unify hundreds of other languages already in use by various military departments and agencies. Interface consideration had been critical in the military's interest in Ada from the start. A High Order Language (HOL) is one that comes close to expressing a program in English, or in algebraic statements. Each line of code is equivalent to what otherwise would be many lines of machine language instructions. Like many other HOL's, Ada programs can run on any computer because they express problems in terms appropriate to the problem, rather than to a particular machine. A portable standard is also expected to save the time and cost of writing multiple versions of the language.[6] The Ada language is reported to be relatively easy to use as compared with other programming languages like Pascal, on which it is based, but it is dependent on an intricate "compiler" to translate HOL into machine code. A member of the Ada design team has said that Ada cannot be expected to be a match for BASIC as an interactive language on a personal computer.[7] Nonetheless, the emphasis on English rather than on technical alpha / numeric vocabulary might have appealed to the translator and expositor of science and mathematics.

"Ada" was not the name the venture first went by when the Department of Defense began soliciting proposals. In the beginning, the project was referred to as "DoD-1," a military designation that many felt would doom its possibilities on the campus and in the marketplace. Draft versions during various stages of

development took on successive names from *The Wizard of Oz*—
Strawman (1975), Woodenman (1976), Tinman (1976). The
names then shifted to industry. There was Ironman (1978), a
version which met the approval of the various armed services
and was sent out for competitive bidding. Steelman (1978)
followed, a document of final language requirements, then
Pebbleman (1978) and Stoneman (1980), documents describing
the Ada programming support environment. Originally nine
hundred companies from fifteen countries entered the competition. A first round reduced the number to seventeen, a second
round to four. The competition was now designated by colors.
On May 2, 1979, the "Green" language, designed by a team
headed by Jean Ichbiah, working for CII [Compagnie Internatio-
nale pour l'Informatique] Honeywell Bull, in Paris, was chosen
as the winner, and Ada was selected as the name in honor of
Lady Lovelace. There may be an ominous parallel, however,
between the lady and the language. Although the U.S. Department of Defense has declared Ada to be its standard, the navy
and air force have standards of their own, and even within the
Pentagon, grumbling has been reported. The British Ministry of
Defense has also mandated Ada in systems as of 1987, but it is
possible that attempts at international standardization will meet
with too much opposition and that the language, like the lady,
might fail before full time. It will also take many years of user
experiences to evaluate capability and effectiveness. The promise, however, is that such embedded software is the most
efficient way for the Department of Defense to modify existing
weapons and to design sophisticated detection, identification,
and precision systems for the future. The idea of her name being
used primarily for military advantage might not have offended
Ada Lovelace. Byron, after all, had ended his days in a war of
liberation, helping the Greeks fight for independence. Moreover, the commercial possibilities of Ada are extensive, and
many civilian applications are already in use.[8]

Notes

INTRODUCTION

1. B 37192.371, Ada to Babbage, July 13, 1843. In this letter Ada says, "I particularly want to know to *what* that is wholly new and valuable you can allude, as being likely to be developed." There is no record that he replied, but as notes "A" and "G" show, she wondered on her own.

   Citations to the Babbage collection of letters in the British Library in London will be referred to hereafter as B followed by the manuscript box number, including folio (official citations begin with "Add." for Catalogue of Additions). Citations to the Lovelace-Byron Collection will be referred to as LB followed by the manuscript box number, including folio. Citations to the Somerville Collection will be referred to by S followed by the manuscript box number, including folio.

   Since 1976, Bodeleian readers have had the benefit of a "Catalogue of the Papers of the Noel, Byron and Lovelace Families," compiled by Mary Clapinson, Senior Assistant Librarian, Department of Western Mss. Elizabeth Patterson has drawn up a more general catalogue for the Somerville Collection.

   Technically, Ada Lovelace was not the first one to write a program for the Analytical Engine, since Babbage himself probably was, but Ada was indeed the first to publish a complex illustration of what such an engine might execute.

2. *Faster Than Thought: A Symposium on Digital Computing Machines* by B. V. Bowden (Lord Bowden, 1964) (New York: Pitman, 1953).

3. In "Lady Lovelace's Notes: Technical Text and Cultural Context" (*Victorian Studies* 28 [Autumn 1984]: 33–67). Dorothy K. Stein argues that Ada's "Notes" present a "misleading and inconsistent" picture of the Analytical Engine and should never have been taken as a "blueprint for scientific development." There is no evidence, however, that Ada or anyone else ever intended the "Notes" to be a "blueprint." Stein's article is part of a larger depreciation, *Ada, A Life and a Legacy* (Cambridge: MIT Press, 1985).

4. It is Lady Lovelace, not Lady Ada, since only daughters of higher ranks such as dukes, marquesses and earls were called by their first name. Thus, Ada's daughter is Lady Anne because Ada's husband was earl of Lovelace.

5. Jack Morrell and Arnold Thackray, *Gentlemen of Science: Early Years of The British Association for the Advancement of Science* (Oxford: Clarendon, 1981), 152.

6. The neighbor was Henry Acland, who wrote to his mother immediately after a "luncheon and ride" with Lord and Lady Lovelace on September 21, 1839. I am indebted to Dr. Harold C. Harley, a resident of Oxford, who called this letter (Bodleian Ms. Acland dep. 22) to my attention. Acland was exactly Ada's age; in 1847 he became secretary of the Oxford meeting of the British Association.

   At the time of his meeting with Ada, she was at Ashley Combe, one of the Lovelace residences, at Porlock Weir, overlooking the Bristol Channel. It was here that she spent some time composing the "Notes." Ashley Combe is only a ruin now, but under Lord Lovelace's direction, it had been expanded and then, under the direction of the second earl of Lovelace, made into an estate in the style of an Italian villa. It was used during World War II as a home for children and demolished in 1966. A gatehouse still stands, with an 1844 keystone, and there are remains of the manor house foundation and stone archways, suggestive now, in their exquisite overgrown decay, of a setting worthy of a Byronic poem.

7. John Cam Hobhouse [Lord Broughton], *Recollections of A Long Life*, ed. Lady Dorchester, 6 vols. (London: John Murray, 1911), 150, 191. The dinner party was on June 15, 1845. The remark by the dinner guest was made at another dinner party, May 15, 1847. Hobhouse first saw Ada early in 1834 and met her again in 1842, an event he recorded as less than pleasant. He found her curt and critical. Eventually, however, she warmed to her father's old comrade, who allegedly had said on Byron's wedding day that he felt as though he were burying his best friend.

8. LB 171.157, Greig to Ada, May 21, 1841.

9. In the *World of Fashion and Continental Feuilletons*, July 8, 1835; noted by Doris Langley Moore in *Ada, Countess of Lovelace: Byron's Legitimate Daughter* (London: John Murray, 1977), 71.

   Notices of Lady Lovelace's death and funeral appeared in the *Times*, November 29, 1852, and December 3, 1852, respectively. These can also be found in S 369. MSBY-13.

10. Canto IV, stanza clxiv.

11. LB 175.123, fragment, August 18, 1852.

12. LB 460, September 6, 1854. *Childe Harold's Pilgrimage. A Romaunt*, 2 vols. (London: John Murray, 1853).

13. Britain's unduly harsh treatment of homosexuals and evidence of Byron's homosexual affairs are presented in *Byron and Greek Love: Homophobia in 19th Century England*, Louis Crompton (Berkeley: University of California Press, 1985).

CHAPTER 1

1. Sketch of the Analytical Engine Invented by Charles Babbage by L. F. Menabrea of Turin, Officer of the Military Engineers [1840], Au Bibliothèque Universelle de Genève, nouvelle serie, xli, October, 1842, no. 82; with notes upon the Memoir by the Translator, ADA AUGUSTA, COUNTESS OF LOVE-

LACE," in *Charles Babbage and His Calculating Engines, Selected Writings by Charles Babbage and Others,* edited and with an introduction by Philip Morrison and Emily Morrison (New York: Dover, 1961), 225–95. Hereafter referred to as "Sketch" and "Notes."

2. Andrew Hodges, *Alan Turing: The Enigma* (New York: Simon and Schuster, 1983), 297n. Hodges makes the remark in specific reference to Ada's account of the generalizing powers of the Analytical Engine. Bletchley Park is in Buckinghamshire, forty-six miles northwest of London.

3. Anthony Hyman. *Charles Babbage: Pioneer of the Computer* (Princeton: Princeton University Press, 1982), 198n.

4. Ada is mentioned in Chapter 8 of *Passages,* in Morrison, *Charles Babbage.*
   Stein argues that Babbage's praise, limited as it was, should be taken as an expression of generosity, not of heartfelt belief (p. 36). She contends that historians of science, relying on Babbage's praise, have mistakenly appreciated the "Notes." It is an argument that assumes extraordinary naïveté or sloppiness on the part of many historians and computer scientists, not to mention Babbage himself, whose supervision of the "Notes," Stein admits, was very close (p. 63).

5. An amusing account of Bowden's discovery of Ada Lovelace and her "Notes" is given in his article "He Invented the Computer—Before Its Time," *Think* 26 (1960): 28–32.

6. The "Notes" originally published in *Taylor's Scientific Memoirs, Selected from Transactions of Foreign Academies of Science and Learned Societies, and from Foreign Journals,* 3, ed. R. Taylor (London: R. and J. Taylor, 1843), 666–731, have been reprinted in a facsimile edition by the Johnson Reprint Corporation (New York, 1966).

7. Brian Randall, ed., "Analytical Engines," in *The Origins of Ditigal Computers: Selected Papers,* 3d. ed. (New York: Springer-Verlag, 1982), introduction.
   Although the Analytical Engine, like the Difference Engine, was designed to be decimal, the use of punched cards suggests the modern binary system.

8. Jeremy Bernstein, *The Analytical Engine: Computers, Past, Present, and Future* (New York: William Morrow; rev. ed., 1981), 65.

9. Allan Bromley, "Charles Babbage's Analytical Engine, 1838," 1981 *Annals of the History of Computing* 4 [1982]: 196–217).

10. In *Glenarvon* (Henry Colburn, publisher, 1816); Lady Caroline was also a mischievous person, and a liar. It was she who in 1816 told Lady Byron "in confidence" that Medora Leigh was Byron's child. The full story is wonderfully narrated in Doris Langley Moore's *The Late Lord Byron.*

11. *Diary* 6:7. He added, however, that she was far from simple: "quite the contrary."

12. Peel (FRS, 1822) was a dedicated friend of science and scientists, despite his cool response to Babbage. (The earlier prime minister, the duke of Wellington, remained a lifelong advocate of the Difference Engine.)

13. The remark was part of Augustus De Morgan's review of C. R. Weld's *History of the Royal Society,* 1848, in the *Atheneum,* October 14, 1848. To Peel's sarcastic remark that the Difference Engine should be set to compute the time at which it would be of use, the *Atheneum* editors responded that it

should be set rather "to compute the number of applications that might remain unanswered before a Minister." Ada wrote Babbage that she found the account "just & impartial," adding "Let the government *answer* it if they can" (B 37194.196; Ada to Babbage, October 18, 1848).

14. She was "alarmed" that it might not be *"accomplished"* (B 37194.197, Ada to Babbage, October 14, 1848). The letters are often difficult to date, especially because she wrote often to family and friends and tended to leave out dates. Good detective work has been done by Moore and others arguing from internal evidence.

15. In a brief comment on the naming of the programming language "Ada," Peter Wegner, of Brown University, writes that he was spurred to check the Biblical Ada in Genesis 4:23–24 ("Ada—The Poetic Connection," *ACM [Association of Computing Machines] Forum* 24 [May, 1981]:239).

> Ada and Zilla, hear my voice:
> Ye wives of Lamech, hearken to my speech;
> For I have slain a man for wounding me,
> And a young man for bruising me.
> If Cain shall be avenged sevenfold,
> Truly Lamech, seventy and sevenfold.

In response, Daniel D. McCracken noted that there was more than one Biblical Ada, beside one of the two wives of the vengeful Lamech, Ada, he pointed out, is also named in Genesis 36, verses 2 and 4, as one of three wives of Esau. "Drawing these strands together, we have this picture of Ada: It is an ornate language of uncertain kinship, destined to be eternal and, in its season, the progenitor of further generations of languages" ("More on the Biblical Origins of Ada" [*ACM Forum* 24 July 1981]: 475).

16. Accounts in *Byron's Letters and Journals*, ed. Leslie A. Marchand, 12 vols. (London: John Murray, 1973–1982), cited hereafter as *Byron's Letters*. Byron to Teresa Guiccioli, October 7, 1820 7:196; Byron to Augusta Leigh, November 6, 1816, 5:110 (he said something similar in a letter to Lady Byron, September 14, 1821).

17. March 4, 1983, in *The Letters of Charles Dickens: The Pilgrim Edition*, eds. Madeline House, Graham Storey, and Kathleen Tillotson (Oxford: Clarendon, 1974). 3:459. The editors speculate that Dickens probably referred to Byron because of Macready, the famous actor, for whom Dickens was helping to get up subscription lists. Byron's play *Werner* was one of Macready's well-known successes.

18. Albany Fonblanque, *The Life and Labours of Albany Fonblanque*, ed. Edward Barrington de Fonblanque (London, 1874), 113.

19. Moore, 6n.

20. Byron to Murray, December 10, 1821. (*Byron's Letters* 9:77).

21. Sophia Frend De Morgan, *Threescore Years and Ten: Reminiscences of the Late . . . De Morgan*, ed. Mary A. De Morgan (London, 1895), 179–80.

22. LB 171.17, Ada to Sophia De Morgan, December 21, [1844]. This letter shows her continued determination to pursue mathematics, despite poor health

and strain. Significantly, the letter concludes with a sigh that she is not pregnant: "*I* can think *anything* better than *that*."

23. LB 118. Entries begin May 14, 1821; the ms. box also contains the notebook Lady Byron kept for Ada.
24. Ibid.
25. Lady Noel to Lady Byron, September 5, 1817; noted by Malcolm Elwin in *Lord Byron's Family: Annabella, Ada, and Augusta, 1816–1824* (London: John Murray, 1975), 167. The letter continues with this devastating report: "Only a few days ago I took her into Your Room, she looked *round* the Bed and *on* the Bed, then into the Closet—seemed disappointed and said 'gone-gone'!"
26. Byron to Lady Byron, March 1, 1816. (*Byron's Letters* 5:39).
27. B. 37192.362, Ada to Babbage, July 10, 1843; S 369 CELE 4, Ada to Agnes Greig, February 5, 1841; LB 41.186, Ada to Lady Byron, November 9, 1840. S 369, CELE 4 also contains copies of Ada's sonnet "The Rainbow."
28. Caroline Fox [Lady George Murray], *Memories of Old Friends*, 2d ed., ed. Horace N. Pym (Philadelphia, 1884), 10.
29. Bryon to Augusta Leigh, October 8, 1823 (*Byron's Letters* 11:47).
30. LB 309 XVI, Lady Byron to Ada, August 10 [1838].
31. De Morgan, *Threescore Years and Ten*, 179–80.
32. Harriet Martineau, *Autobiography* ed. Maria Weston Chapman, 2 vols. (Boston, 1877), 1:298.
33. Fox, 183. She did read it.
34. Fonblanque, 1:13.
35. Byron to Tom Moore, February 2, 1818 (*Byron's Letters* 11:197). Restored from the ms. Journal. Was Byron aware of all the implications of his reference one year later when he called Ada his "little Electra" and Lady Byron "the moral Clytemnestra"? No doubt.
36. Byron to Lady Melbourne, October 18, 1812 (*Byron's Letters* 2:231); to Annabella Milbanke, November 10, 1812 (*Byron's Letters* 3:159).
37. Lady Byron to Mrs. Villiers [Hon. Mrs. George (née Theresa Parker) Villiers], March 24, 1817, in Elwin, 139; Lady Byron to Dr. King, LB 77.33, January 7, 1829; LB 737, January 20, 1829.
38. LB 42, 12 & 14, Ada to Lady Byron, February 24, 1841.
39. B 37189.281, Ada to Babbage, January 18, 1836.
40. Hobhouse 5:290.
41. LB 162.5, William King to Ada, June 9, 1835.

CHAPTER 2

1. Ironically, so would Herman Hollerith look to Jacquard. Hollerith, an engineer who is considered the father of electronic computers, must have had "constructive knowledge" of Babbage, his biographer, Geoffrey Austrian, writes, but Hollerith drew directly on Jacquard for his own models (Geoffrey D. Austrian, Letter to the author, June 2, 1984). Austrian is the author of *Herman Hollerith* (New York: Columbia University Press, 1982).

2. Carl Boyer. *A History of Mathematics* (New York: John Wiley, 1968), 621.

3. Morrell and Thackray, 257.

4. Although the classical tripos for language and literature was established in 1824, it did not lead to an honors degree. The 1852 report led to the 1856 bill of reform, which abolished religious tests for degrees in all fields other than divinity.

5. S Dep. 367, box 17, Ada to Greig; December 5, 1844, contains her statement that Lord Lovelace joined on her account.

6. Martha McMackin Garland. *Cambridge Before Darwin: The Ideal of a Liberal Education, 1800–1860* (Cambridge: Cambridge University Press, 1980), 5–7.

7. Elizabeth Chambers Patterson. *Mary Somerville and the Cultivation of Science, 1815–1840* (Boston: Martinus Nijhoff, 1983), 90.

8. John Theodore Merz, *History of European Scientific Thought in the 19th Century,* 4 vols. (Gloucester, Mass.:, Peter Smith, 1896; rpt. 1976), 1:297.

9. Hyman, 43–44, 50, 1–2.

10. M. R. Williams. "The Difference Engines," *Computer Journal* 19 (February 1, 1976): 82.

11. Hodges, 61.

12. Hyman, 53; Morrell and Thackray, 49.

13. Williams discovered the work of J. H. Müller, a captain of engineers in the Hessian army whose plan for a third difference engine was described in a 1786 book by one E. Lipstein. According to this account, Müller, like Babbage, planned both to calculate and to print out. Williams adds that it is "almost certain" that Babbage did not know about Müller (Williams, 83).

14. B 37192.352, Ada to Babbage, July 5, 1843. Specifically, she questioned the nature of his views on pages 96–97, where Babbage analogized between the Difference Engine and the Deity ("Argument from Laws Intermitting on the Nature of Miracles," chapter 8 of the *Treatise*). In an appendix note, Babbage made it clear that it was an Analytical Engine he was beginning to think about, as a result of these Bridgewater speculations.

15. Garland, 12. Incidentally, it was Ada's expressed hope at the time to have "knowledge enough" in order to review Whewell's books. (B 37192.339, Ada to Babbage, July [3], 1843).

16. Merz, 277–78.

17. Walter F. Cannon, "Scientists and Broad Churchmen: An Early Victorian Intellectual Network," *Journal of British Studies* 4 (1964): 67.

18. William Whewell, "On the Connexion of the Physical Sciences," *Quarterly Review* 51 (1834): 53.

19. Merz, 232.

20. E. J. Hobsbawm, *The Age of Revolution: Europe, 1789–1848* (London: Weidenfeld & Nicolson, 1962), 278.

21. Garland, 15.

22. Cannon, 76. The Panizzi and Babbage "Speculation," by Robert M. Hayes, in the *Journal of Library History* 20 (Spring 1985), 179–85, was called to my attention by Rosannah Cole, at the Carl H. Pforzheimer Library. Since Anthony Panizzi (1797–1879) had been asked in 1832 to develop a class or subject catalogue for the library of the Royal Society, a venture he postponed

and that cost him much pain, Hayes wonders, "Did Babbage know Panizzi? And did they ever discuss the possibilities for the use of Babbage's analytical engine in Panizzi's operational problems in producing catalog in the British Museum?" (181). Indeed, the answer is that they did know each other, or of each other's work: "I am very anxious to have the growing records of that office [clearing house] preserved . . ." (B 36717.538, Babbage to Panizzi, July 28, 1856).

23. LB 67.19, Lady Byron to Augustus De Morgan, September 3, 1856.

CHAPTER 3

1. LB 172.125, Ada to Dr. King, March 9, 1834; LB 172.133, Ada to Dr. King, March 24, 1834; LB 172.133-4, Dr. King to Ada, April 24, 1834; LB 172.133, Ada to Dr. King, March 24, 1834; LB 172.125, Ada to Dr. King, March 9, 1834; LB 172.128, Dr. King to Ada, March 15, 1834.

2. Sir Frederick Pollock to Augustus De Morgan, August 7, 1869, in W.W. Rouse Ball, *A History of the Study of Mathematics at Cambridge* (London, 1889), 111–13. It was Pollock who said he was "not up to the differential calculus."

3. Frida Knight, *University Rebel: The Life of William Frend, 1757–1841* (London: Victor Gollancz, 1971), 275.

4. Helena M. Pycior, "At the Intersection of Mathematics and Humor: Lewis Carroll's Alices and Symbolical Algebra," *Victorian Studies* 28 (Fall 1984): 153.

5. B 37192.370, Ada to Babbage, July 13, 1843. Stein says that Ada's question is a "curious one" (p. 53), since she should have known about negative and imaginary numbers from discussion with De Morgan and Babbage. Stein accuses Ada of "falsehood" by saying in the "Notes" that she had no chance of inquiring into how the machine would handle such "numbers." But Ada might have been referring to the satisfaction of an answer. Stein concedes that a response from Babbage does not survive and that there is no way to know how adequate it might have been, given his illness in the autumn of 1842 and his usual pressures.

6. Patterson, *Mary Somerville*, 149.

7. De Morgan, *Threescore Years and Ten*, 31. Mascheroni is known today for showing that Euclidean constructions need only a compass, rather than a compass and a straightedge. I am indebted for this observation to Prof. Joseph P. Malkevitch, of the Department of Mathematics, York College, CUNY.

8. Martinaeu 1:270.

9. LB 165.2, Ada to William King, June 8, 1835. The love of both music and mathematics, not uncommon to mathematicians, meets its exception in Charles Babbage.

10. Morrell and Thackray, 423.

11. Men and women both contributed to the *Ladies' Diary*, as contributors' lists show (although many women chose to sign only their initials or to use male names). Most of the women were self-taught, and many were the wives of mathematicians. See Teri Perl, "The *Ladies' Diary* or *Woman's Almanac, 1704–*

1841," Historica Mathematica 6 (1979): 36–53; and Ruth and Peter Wallis, "Female Philomaths." *Historica Mathematica 7* (1980), 57–64.

12. Quoted by Merz 1:236; from the *Edinburgh Review*. Pycior also refers to its "significant mathematical content" (158).

13. Morrell and Thackray, 148ff.

14. Patterson, *Mary Somerville*, 138.

15. Quoted by Merz 1:237.

16. It is odd, therefore, that Ada would indeed make a serious error in her translation of Menabrea, one that Stein argues is indicative of Ada's mathematical ignorance. In writing "cos." (cosine) for "cas" (case)—a change in punctuation as well as in vowel—Ada certainly translated nonsense. Stein notes that the error is corrected without comment in Bowden's edition. One comment might have been to the effect that Babbage himself didn't notice it. See discussion in chapter 5.

17. An observation in a footnote by Velma R. and Harry D. Huskey, "Lady Lovelace and Charles Babbage, *Annals of the History of Computing* 2 (October 1980): 325. The letter calling her his "interpreter" is LB 168.50, Babbage to Ada, September 9, 1843.

18. S Dep. c 355, MSAU-2, "34," 31. A first-draft autobiography is in Mrs. Somerville's hand; a second draft, MSAU-3, is also in the manuscript box.

19. S MSDIP-18, Dep. Box II, "26." Mrs. Butler was the editor. The Patterson article is in the same box (138–40). The letter is dated May 10, 1869.

20. David Spencer, *London Times* (August 7, 1984), 8.

21. Stein insists that letters to De Morgan, 1841 to 1842, show Ada "wrestling with a simple and straightforward problem in functional equations, still unable to grasp the technique of substituting a new expression back into an equation, even when the correct formula to substitute has been handed to her." She adds that Ada had similar trouble with Mrs. Somerville and with Dr. King. However, some functional equations, such as those involving two variables, are messy to handle; besides, difficulty with algebra is not a litmus test of theoretical comprehension or imagination.

A problem with Stein's analysis is that parts, at times, add up to apparent contradictions. Arguing that Ada never went beyond elementary exercises, Stein then allows that Ada was able to take exception to parts of De Morgan's calculus text and even offer improvements. If Babbage was misguided in not accepting the concept of limits, and De Morgan knew better, then it would follow that Ada was not entirely the overreaching amateur Stein makes her out to be. De Morgan, Stein writes, "must have been delighted at Ada's grasping the idea that a two-dimension treatment [of complex numbers] can be generalized into three dimensions or more" (p. 80). It seems hard to believe that because Ada's metaphysical turn of mind found sympathetic response in De Morgan, he overlooked her ignorance and superficiality, dazzled and mystified by her as he was along with so many specialists, then and now. Indeed, later on (p. 102), Stein says that Ada might have learned about the development of modern algebra from De Morgan and Babbage.

22. LB 344, Augustus De Morgan to Lady Byron, January 21, 1844.

23. Stein counters by saying that De Morgan was being unfair to Mrs. Somerville because her position was a respectable one for the time (p. 83), and that what De Morgan meant was that Ada would have demanded a less sophisticated explanation in words, while Mrs. Somerville, secure and expert, would have been content with a mathematical description. Again, the problem is *parti pris:* the fact is that the notation is not for force, and hindsight argument from the age of particle physics (a tack taken by Stein here and elsewhere) seems unfair.

24. LB 67.127, Lady Byron to Augustus De Morgan, January 20, 1844.

25. B 37191.87, Ada to Babbage, [1839]. The same language appears in a letter (LB 168.38, Babbage to Ada, November 29, 1839) in which Babbage tells her that her tastes for mathematics are "so decided" that she ought to pursue the subject. He also announces that he has just thought of an "improvement" for the (Analytical) Engine that might set his drawings back months.

26. A particularly beautiful calculating machine is the Second Empire piano arithomometer, by Charles Xavier Thomas de Cohmar (1855), an elaborate piece in gold. This model, the Pascal, the Leibniz, and replicas of both the Difference Engine and the mill portion of the Analytical Engine are on display in the IBM Antique Calculator Collection, in New York.

27. Martineau, 300; she visited Coleridge in 1834, shortly before his death.

28. LB 309, 336, Lady Byron to Dr. William King, June 7 and June 21, 1833. In addition to having been Ada's tutor, Dr. King was also one of Lady Byron's doctors.

   Lady Byron's view of Babbage can also be seen in her ambivalent attitude towards his *Ninth Bridgewater Treatise,* which she mentioned as an important but disappointing work, the result of writing too quickly.

29. LB 168.35, Babbage to Ada, June 10, 1835.

30. Sophia Frend De Morgan, *Memoirs of Augustus De Morgan* (London, 1882), 89.

31. Bowden, 10, 34. The process is "in use today in all parallel computers," computers that allow for simultaneous computations.

32. LB 168.26, Ada to Lady Annabella Acheson, November 10, 1834. The ms. box contains several letters to Annabella, written on Cambridge Scribbling Paper, the "official" paper for mathematical exercises.

33. Williams's very fine explanations, 82–83. Müller's plans, incidentally, called for a third order of difference.

34. As Brian Randall points out (p. 3), Pascal, long considered the first to have used the idea of linked gear wheels for an adding machine, was probably antedated by Wilhelm Shickland, a German astronomer.

35. Alan G. Bromley, "Inside the World's First Computers," *New Scientist* 99 September 15, 1983), 781–84.

36. Garry John Tee, "The Heritage of Charles Babbage in Australasia," *Annals of the History of Computing* 5 (1983): 45–59. Tee has traced manuscripts to the Wanganui Regional Museum. Babbage's son Benjamin Herschel Babbage (1815–1878) had gone to live in New South Wales in 1851. Tee's article is adapted from a May 13, 1981, lecture given before the Second Australasian Mathematical Convention at the Uinversity of Sydney.

Babbage described the demonstration model of the Difference Engine on June 14, 1822, in a note before the Astronomical Society. One month later (July 3), in a note to Sir Humphry Davy, then president of the Royal Society, Babbage was proposing a much larger version. In 1827–1828 he was in Europe studying factories and workshops. The portion on view at the London Science Museum was put together in 1832. Babbage numbered his machines, but it is still not easy to put models, parts, and plans in chronological order. The Difference Engine now in the Science Museum in London was originally given by Babbage to the museum of King's College, London, where it sat for twenty years. Babbage had insisted that the government owned the machine, an insistence that he thought would necessitate its being funded again.

Williams argues that the government got its money's worth out of Babbage because innovations for improving workshops, training, and mechanical notation porved valuable later on in the cotton-spinning industry and in the production of new tables.

37. Hyman, 134.
38. Bowden, "He Invented the Computer," 30.
39. Martineau, 268.
40. Hyman, 195.

CHAPTER 4

1. LB 42.152, Ada to Lady Byron, November 11, 1844.
2. B 37191.566, Ada to Babbage, February 22, 1841.
3. LB 171.153, Ada to Greig, May 15, 1841.
4. LB 171.8, Ada to Sophia De Morgan, March 1, 1841. The letter begins, "Read this to *yourself* first."
5. LB 163.38, Babbage to Ada, November 29, 1839. The 1839 letter from Ada to Babbage (B 37191.87) in which she mentions her decided taste has no specific date.

   Although Stein's point that Ada had not really kept up with Babbage's changing plans from 1835 to 1842 is well taken, a case could be made that no one could have kept up, and that, until recently, no one even knew the extent of Babbage's plans and revisions for his engines.
6. B 37191.532, Ada to Babbage, January 5, 1841. The letter ends on a mysterious note. Ada has just asked Babbage to put her in possession of the main points of the Analytical Engine. A dash follows, then: "I have more reasons than one for desiring this."

   Those who believe that Ada and Babbage were involved in a mathematical scheme to bet on the horses note oblique references to a "book" in the Lovelace-Babbage correspondence. However, as Doris Langley Moore suggests, the book may well have been Ada's mathematical scrapbook. Babbage and Ada often wrote in shorthand, and cryptic remarks, nicknames, and fragmented conversation do not in themselves mean that occasional references to "the book" refer to bookmaking. Moreover, the sending back and forth of a mathematics book would not be unusual, as Mrs. Moore also points out, given Babbage's desire to promote the interests of his young assistant and her concern to promote herself with visiting scientists.

The strongest argument against the idea that Babbage and Ada would have tried to use probability theory to win at the track is not that such activity would have been out of character, but that it would have been beyond the capacity of the Difference Engine. Ada and Babbage may have toyed with a betting scheme, but there is little to recommend their having given it serious thought and attention. Besides, when she finally took to betting on horses, Ada lost a great deal of money—no reason to stop gambling, to be sure, but one at least to cause doubt about the efficacy of a "system."

Stein's conjectures, that the "book" refers to a "coauthored work in progress" with Babbage, a "more detailed and complete elaboration of the practical possibilities and philosophical implications of the Analytical Engine," are unsupported (*A Life*, p. 122).

7. B 37192.422, Ada to Babbage, August 14, 1843; LB 476, Ada to Lady Byron, August 8, 1843. The irritation with Babbage was genuine though short-lived.
8. LB 42.4, 8, 9, Ada to Lady Byron, January 11, 1841.
9. LB 41.179, Ada to Lady Byron, July 30, 1840.
10. LB 42.29, Ada to Lady Byron, March 3, 1841. "Revelations to Her Daughter," appendix 3, in Moore, 372–73; the date of the letter is February 27, 1841.
11. LB 166.3, 4, 5, 209, Ada to Lord Lovelace, April 1842, LB 165.209, n.d. but approximately the same period.
12. Ada repeats the motto in B 37192.352, Ada to Babbage, July [5], 1843. She has been working "doggedly" on the Bernouilli numbers, grappling with the subject and connecting it with others. She intends to take in succession other subjects. " '*Labor ipse voluptas*' is in *very* deed my motto!" (Ada to Andrew Crosse). The letter to Crosse was part of the group published in excerpted form in the *Argosy* 8 (1869) under the heading "Byron's Daughter."
13. S d 367, MSBY-9, "17," Ada to Greig, December 16, 1842.
14. De Morgan, *Memoirs* 34.
15. Fox, 9.
16. "Byron's Daughter," 358.
17. De Morgan, *Three Score Years and Ten*, 179.
18. "I have documented evidence that Lady Byron read the following poems: *Giaour, Don Juan, Corsair, Hebrew Melodies* and *Childe Harold* [cantos I & II]. She probably read most of his poetry. She stated in a letter to Lady Melbourne dated 12th Feburary 1814, 'He may without exaggeration be compared to Shakespeare' " (Letter to the author from Miss Lucy I. Edwards, M.B.E., West Bridgford Nottingham, September 1, 1984).
19. *Byron's Letters* 9:127n.
20. B 37192.409, Ada to Babbage, July 30, 1843.
21. Frank D. McConnell, ed. *Byron's Poetry: A Norton Critical Edition*. (New York: Norton, 1978), 205n.

22. LB 42.138, Ada to Lady Byron, [date uncertain]. Ada refers to "dawning anticipations" about Anne's character, however, so it is likely to have been written when her daughter was a few years old. Mary Clapinson places the letter in the early 1840s.

23. Ada to Babbage, B 37192.393, July 27, 1843; B 37192.339, July [3] 1843. Ada made similar statements to her mother during the same period.

24. Martineau, 269–70.

25. "Vestiges of the Natural History of Creation," a review, in the Edinburgh Review 82 (July 1845): 4. Many names were suggested for authorship, among them Prince Albert's, and even Darwin's, but it was Darwin who identified Chambers.

26. Fonblanque, 113.

27. Hobhouse 6:175–76, June 3, 1846; 6:145, May 23, 1845.

28. B 37192.350, Ada to Babbage, July 5, 1843.

29. B 37192.335, Ada to Babbage, July [2], 1843. The word genius was still predominantly used in its etymological sense as native gift or talent, rather than in the primary sense today of extraordinary intelligence. The distinction was between what was natural and what was acquired.

30. B 37192.347, Ada to Babbage, July [4], 1843.

31. LB 41.126, 127, Ada to Lady Byron, July 25, 1843.

CHAPTER 5

1. LB 42.88, Ada to Lord Lovelace, July 28, 1843.

2. Attempting to diminish Ada's importance, Stein argues that Ada and Menabrea were "relative novices"—young, inexperienced, and too impressed by Babbage's genius to temper their enthusiasm and question Babbage's optimistic claims (p. 56). Yet, Menabrea was thirty-three when his article on the Analytical Engine was published in 1842, and Ada was twenty-eight when the "Notes" were published—a mature age for those working in mathematics. One may ask why either Menabrea or Ada should have challenged Babbage when he was busy challenging himself, constantly changing plans. Perhaps the "Notes" should have been called "On Work in Progress." For example, drawings show that Babbage was considering means other than punched cards to do the programming.

3. Stein, 63.

4. Stein points out that Ada emphasized prototype programs, which are of no particular interest today, while mentioning only in passing the ability of the engine to change course, contingent on results of intermediate stages (p. 49). The charge depends upon the view (not mine) that the "Notes" have been taken as a blueprint for computer development.

5. Sylvie Breaud, "Ada, Analyste et Metaphysicienne." Pénélope, Publication du Group d'Etudes feministes de l'Université Paris (1984), 22.

6. Stein gives as evidence of Ada's continuous reliance on Babbage the borrowing of a "capital" metaphor from Babbage's 1832 Economy of Machinery and Manufactures: "In the case of the Analytical Engine we have undoubtedly to

lay out a certain capital of analytical labour in one particular line . . ." (p. 94). The very same word, however, turns up in Ada's letters to Greig and Sophia written two years before the "Notes," proving only what is obvious—that Ada served Babbage, not the other way around, and that Ada tended to use the same words and expressions in her extensive correspondence.

7. Hyman, 198.

8. Ibid., 26.

9. Although Stein argues that Babbage encouraged Ada and Menabrea to claim they had not sufficient time to discuss matters with him (a move that freed all around from responsibility), and that Babbage did not really admire Ada to the extent his infrequent statements indicate, the argument depends upon readers being convinced that Babbage was completely taken in by Lady Lovelace and that a century of historians of mathematics were as gullible.

10. B 37192.414, Ada to Babbage, August 1, 1843.

11. Velma R. Huskey and Harry D. Huskey, "Ada, Countess of Lovelace, and Her Contribution to Computing," *Abacus* 1 (Winter 1984): 27.

12. B 37192.44, Ada to Babbage, July 4, 1843. Stein disparages Ada as a "fairy" waving her wand or hands, unaware of the full extent of Babbage's difficulties in trying to create an algebraic machine (p. 45) There is no doubt that Ada did not fully understand problems connected with the Analytical Engine; not even Babbage understood them.

The "fairy" reference has also led to romantic speculation about "Puzzle-pate" and the "Philosopher." The seductive expression was all on her side, but it was only style. Other flirtations were more provocative, and Ada wrote Babbage about at least one of them. A Mr. Frederick Knight, from Somersetshire, a "very delightful" man, she was pleased to report, was still calling her his "ladye-love," though she had been away for a while. "Am I very naughty to send you such a calling up of dubious speculations & associations?" she teased Babbage.

A newspaper of the time confirmed what Woronzow Greig had sensed two years earlier: Lady Lovelace, it now appeared, was "flirting [with a man] rather boldly and with a Byronic lack of discretion" (item cited by Moore, p. 160). In a letter to the author, Moore says the newspaper cannot be identified.

Ada Lovelace was not Babbage's only intellectual consort among the ladies, though she was his favorite and the most talented. Ironically, the "Notes" are a cold report of their relationship, and *Passages* hardly notices her. She had been dead for many years by then, her disgrace and scandal kept for the most part from the general public. Perhaps Babbage felt that the less said the better, for her own sake and, of course, for that of his beloved engines.

13. B 37192.388, Ada to Babbage, July 25, 1843.

14. Stein, 45. The extent of Ada's mathematics most certainly would have revealed to her the impossibility of the concept expressed as cos. $n = \infty$. On July 30, she writes to Babbage that the printer has made an error in setting the expression $(a + bx') \times (A + B \cos 'x)$, and she asks him, once again, to

check her copy. Ada sent "Note E" in sections, and it is not inconceivable that drafts were confused with revises and that errors were overlooked. If denigration is to depend on the evidence of minor error, then, by Stein's own fact-finding (chapter 3, n. 12), H. P. Babbage should be indicted and the Morrisons as well, the son for inexplicably changing an infinity sign (the horizontal figure eight) to $1/o$, a trigonometric notation standing for undefined, rather than infinity, and the Morrisons for reprinting it. (Stein, p. 303)

Ada's French was excellent. She thought Menabrea's style "clear and masterly," and the whole a "striking production," as she wrote in the "Notes." But she was not entirely an invisible translator. She points out an "apparent discrepancy" in two passages where Menabrea is discussing the four arithmetic operations that a Pascal-type calculator and the Analytical Engine can both perform. She clarifies, and then indicates differences between the Pascal and the Analytical Engine in dealing with the four operations, noting that in the engine the operations are starting points, the ultimate goal of which is the *"subsequent combination of these* in every possible way." The apparent discrepancy, she says, much stronger in the translation, is owing to "it's being impossible to render precisely into the English tongue all the niceties of distinction which the French idiom happens to admit of in the phrases used for the two passages."

15. Bowden, "A Brief History," Preface.
16. B 37192.362, Ada to Babbage, [July 10, 1843]. She also asks to see the report of the Royal Society on the Difference Engine. She may not have been that mathematically experienced, but she was determined to do her homework.
17. Randall, 14.
18. The article "Ada, Countess of Lovelace, and her Contribution to Computing" by the Huskeys contains a summary of Ada's work on notes "D" and "G."

CHAPTER 6

1. *Taylor's Scientific Memoirs* 3: 39, 666–731. The Johnson facsimile reprint is ten pages shorter than the Dover publication.

   A partial account of the engine appeared in a portion of a "Letter to [L.A.J.] Quetelet" (1796–1874), the Belgian statistician and astronomer, whom Babbage had met in 1830 and invited to the British Association. It appeared in the same Taylor volume as Ada's "Notes." Babbage had written the letter in May 1835, and its brief description of the engine reflected work he had been doing since October of the previous year. His paper, "On the Mathematical Power of the Calculating Engine," written in December 1837, the year he switched from barrel mechanisms to punched cards for sequence control, is considered very difficult (see Bromley).

2. Four uncatalogued letters from Ada to Richard Taylor (August 1843, St. Bride Printing Office, London). According to James Mosley, the librarian at St. Bride, "the firm had some difficulty in securing payment" (letter to the author, July 25, 1984).

3. LB 42.98, 100, 102, Ada to Lady Byron, Summer 1843.
4. LB 171.44, 45, Faraday to Ada, October 24, 1843; also Moore, 218. Babbage had sent Faraday a copy of the translation and "Notes." On September 1, 1843, Faraday wrote Babbage, thanking him but indicating that he really couldn't understand it. The "it," however, was the translation, which Faraday assured Babbage that he could "well understand by its effects upon those who do understand it how great a work it is."
5. LB 174.95. Mrs. Somerville to Ada, February 5, 1844. Stein dismisses Mrs. Somervile's praise as faint and distant, but offers no hard evidence for her suggestion that it was insincere.
6. M 5590.22, Ada to Babbage, [September 28, 1843]. Ms. is in the Nottingham Public Library. Reference is courtesy of Miss Lucy I. Edwards, M.B.E.
7. Elizabeth Barrett Browning to Robert Browning, February 17, 1845, in *Letters of Robert and Elizabeth Barrett Browning: 1845–1846*, 2 vols. ed. Elvan Kitner (Cambridge: Harvard University Press, 1968), 1: 23–24.
8. *Philosophical Magazine* (September 1843), 245. One year after his death, the British Association was still debating the engines. In 1872 it was reported that the successful realization of Babbage's design "might mark an epoch in the history of computation equally memorable with that of the introduction of logarithms" (*Report* [1878], 100). Construction of the engine was not advised, however, owing, it was said, to lack of information in the plans as to cost, strength, and durability.
9. Weld, 386–87.
10. LB 166.75, Ada to Lord Lovelace, [1843]. The long letter from Ada to Babbage is B 37192.422, August 14, 1843.
11. B 37194.340, Ada to Babbage, July [3], 1843. She was also not apparently familiar with the intended publication, the *Philosophical Magazine*, since she asks Babbage if it reviews books.
12. S c 367, MSBY-9, "17," Ada to Greig, November 15, 1844; LB 166.159, Ada to Lord Lovelace, November 29, 1844. See also Moore, 215–16. Ada indicated that a prime motive in this endeavor would be to explore her own condition and the effects of mesmerism.
13. LB 339, Augustus De Morgan to Lady Byron, January 21, 1844.
14. In volume 4:92 of the *Royal Society of London Catalogue of Scientific Papers*, Lady Lovelace is noted as the translator of Mitscherlich, but this listing is a transcription error. A letter from Wheatstone to Ada indicates that he had proposed she do a translation of August Ludwig Seebeck's memoir in the *Transactions* of the Berlin Academy. Although she did not do it, she obviously toyed with the idea to some extent: two brief paragraphs on Seebeck are in her papers and begin: "If we now turn from the external to the internal existence of Seebeck, and to the consideration of what he has advanced. . . ." It is suggested that Ada was considering an evaluation of Seebeck's work against the "revival of physical science going on at the start of his career" (LB 175.222).

   Volume 4 (1846) of *Taylor's Scientific Memoirs* contains Seebeck's 1836 paper "Remarks on the Polarization of Light by Reflexion," but efforts to discover who did the translation have been unavailing. Taylor's account books are incomplete. The notes on Seebeck are in LB 175.222. As Mary Clapinson points out, the ms. box "contains several other fragments in Ada's hand, and (fols. 211–17) a draft review of a pamphlet by William Gregory on von Reichenbach's work on magnetism." Mrs. Clapinson adds that as far as she is able to determine, "there are no letters of Mitscherlich and Edward Sabine among Ada's papers here" (letter to the author, October 5, 1984).

Ada also wrote a set of mathematical footnotes to Lord Lovelace's essay "On Climate in Connection with Husbandry, with reference to a work entitled 'Cours d'agriculture, par le Comte de Gasparin,' " which was published in December 1848 in the *Journal of the Royal Agricultural Society.* Stein amply covers the content and correspondence surrounding the review but, again, seems to present ambiguous evidence of Ada's lack of mathematical knowledge (see chapter 4).

15. LB 166.159, Ada to Lord Lovelace, November 29, 1844.
16. Moore, 160.
17. LB 166.159, Ada to Lord Lovelace, November 29, 1844.
18. LB 373, Lord Lovelace to Lady Byron, June 25, 1850.
19. Murray ms., June 14, 1846; see Moore, 240–41.
20. LB 43.122, Ada to Lady Byron, September 15, 1850.
21. Reportedly taken down by [Edward] Blaquière, member of the London Greek Committee (Marchand 3:1227).
22. LB 46.253, Lord Lovelace to Lady Byron, January 6, 1853; LB 46.243-4, Lord Lovelace to Lady Byron, December 17, 1852.
23. Quoted by Moore, 299.
24. LB 43.246, Ada to Lady Byron, October 29, 1851.
25. B 37197.215, Babbage to Ockham, June 14, 1857.
26. J. M. Dubbey, a mathematician, probably expresses contemporary judgment when he writes that "most of Lady Lovelace's notes are elaborations on the points made by Menabrea. . . ." His own account of the Analytical Engine gives more attention to the Menabrea article than to the annotation (*The Mathematical Work of Charles Babbage* [Cambridge: Cambridge University Press, 1978], chapter 8).
27. Hyman, 178.
28. B 37192.350, Ada to Babbage, July 5, 1843. Ada had begun by saying it was Lord Lovelace who joked about what a *"General"* she would make.
29. Ibid. I am suggesting that this was the reason for the estrangement that Lovelace had in mind. Even if a particular event—such as Lady Byron's belated discovery of the extent of Ada's gambling and its financial consequences—seems more likely as a proximate reason, a strong case could still be made for Byron as the ultimate and underlying cause.

APPENDIX 1

1. In *Memories of Old Friends* (1835–1837), Caroline Fox reports that Byron presented the poem to Lady Byron by wrapping it up in a number of unpaid bills and flinging it at her in the room where she was sitting (p. 9).
2. Written in Switzerland, May–June 1816.

APPENDIX 2

1. S 368 MSBY, Lovelace to Greig.
2. Morrell and Thackray, 508–9.
3. Robert Lee, "Of the Malignant Disease of the Uterus," *Cyclopaedia of Practical Medicine*, 5 vols., ed. John Forbes, Alexander Tweedie, John Conolly; rev. ed. by Robley Duglison (Philadelphia, 1854) 4:613–20. I am indebted to Dr. Lewis Thomas, President Emeritus of Memorial Sloan-Kettering Cancer Center, for calling this work to my attention.
4. M. Jeanne Peterson, *The Medical Profession in Mid-Victorian London* (Berkeley: University of California Press, 1978), chapter 1.

APPENDIX 3

1. Letter to the author, June 15, 1984.
2. Martin Gardner, *The Annotated Snark* (New York: Simon & Schuster, 1962). The original publication, with nine illustrations by Henry Holiday, was published in London, in 1876.

   There was a definite relationship between Dodgson and De Morgan, however. Both published works on the fifth book of Euclid's *Elements (1836 and 1868, respectively), and Dodgson referred to De Morgan in his Symbolic Logic.* Dodgson also knew Peacock but never accepted symbolic algebra. See Pycior.
3. Vladimir Nabokov, *Ada or Ardor: A Family Chronicle* (New York: McGraw-Hill, 1969).
4. Romulus Linney, *Childe Byron, A play in Two Acts,* Produced in New York in 1981 at the Circle Repertory Theater, the play was directed by Marshall W. Mason and starred William Hurt as Byron and Lindsay Crouse as both Ada and Lady Byron.

APPENDIX 4

1. Tee, 48.
2. Pascal, Euler, Gauss, and Cantor also got languages.
3. News release, Office of the Assistant Secretary of Defense (Public Affairs), Washington, D.C., February 9, 1981, OX5-0192.
4. James Fawcette, "Ada Tackles Software Bottleneck," *High Technology* 3 (February 1983): 50. It also provides other data types, such as records for file processing, access for pointing to other data objects, and enumeration for grouping data elements not necessarily numeric.
5. The line of succession is complicated. I am indebted to Mary Clapinson for setting the record straight. She writes that the link between Ada Lovelace and the Lyttons came in 1889,

   . . . when the 3rd Earl of Lytton married Judith Baroness Wentworth. Judith was the only daughter of Ada's daughter, Lady Anne Blunt. The title of Wentworth could pass through the female line and went from Lady Byron to Ralph (Ada's son), to his daughter Ada. When this second

Ada died in June 1917 the title went (very briefly) to her aunt, Lady Anne Blunt, who died in December of the same year, when Judith became Baroness Wentworth. The present [sic] fourth Lord Lytton is Judith's son, and inherited the additional title of Baron Wentworth on her death in 1957.* The Lovelace-Byron papers, in essence Lady Byron's and Ada's papers, descended with the Wentworth title. The Lovelace title moved away from Ada's descendants, when her son Ralph died without a son. It descended through the male line to Ralph's step-brother. (letter to the author, October 15, 1984).

[*The fifth Lord Lytton succeeded to the title in January 1985.]

In a letter to the author, October 18, 1984, the late Lord Lytton writes that his lifelong pursuit of defence disposed him to view the naming of the Ada language with delight. In January 1985, upon the death of his father, who was fourth earl of Lytton, Viscount Knebworth succeeded to the title.

6. B. A. Wichmann, "Is Ada Too Big? A Designer Answers the Critics," ACM 27 (Feburary 1984): 98–103. Called to my attention by T. C. Wu, Department of Mathematics, York College, Cuny.

7. Fawcette, 49.

8. R. M. Blasewitz, "Ada—Not Just Another Programming Language," RCA Engineer 29 (1984): 24–31.

List of Works Cited

Atheneum (October 14, 1848); 1029–30. "Mr. Babbage's Calculating Machine."

Austrian, Geoffrey D. *Herman Hollerith*. New York: Columbia University Press, 1982.

———. Letter to the author, June 2, 1984.

Babbage, Charles. "Addition to the Memoir of M. Menabrea on the Analytical Engine." *Scientific Memoirs* 3:xii, 666. In *The London, Edinburgh, and Dublin Philosophical Magazine and Journal of Science* 23 (1843): 234–39.

———. *Passages from the Life of a Philosopher*. [See entry under Morrison.]

Ball, W. W. Rouse. *A History of the Study of Mathematics at Cambridge*. London, 1889.

Bernstein, Jeremy. *The Analytical Engine: Computers Past, Present, and Future*. New York: William Morrow, 1981. [Originally these six essays appeared in the *New Yorker* magazine.]

Blasewitz, R. M. "Ada—Not Just Another Programming Language." *RCA Engineer* 29 (1984): 23–31.

Bloor, David. "Hamilton and Peacock on the Essence of Algebra." In *Social History of Nineteenth-Century Mathematics*, edited by Herbert Mehrtens, Henk Bos, and Ivo Schneider, 202–32. Boston: Birkhäuser, (1981).

Bowden, B. V. "A Brief History of Computation." In *Faster Than Thought: A Symposium on Digital Computing Machines*, 3–31. New York: Pitman, (1953).

———. "He Invented the Computer—Before Its Time." *Think* 26 (1960): 28–32.

Boyer, Carl. *A History of Mathematics*. New York: John Wiley, 1968.

Breaud, Sylvie. "Ada, Analyste et Metaphysicienne." *Pénélope pour l'histoire des femmes*. Paris: Publication du Group d'Etudes Feministes de l'Université Paris, (1983), 22–25.

Bromley, Alan G. "Charles Babbage's Analytical Engine, 1838." *Annals of the History of Computing* 4 (1982): 196–217.

———. "Inside the World's First Computers." *New Scientist* 99 (September 15, 1983): 781–84.

"Byron's Daughter." *Argosy* 8 (1869): 358–61.

Cannon, Walter F. "Scientists and Broad Churchmen: An Early Victorian Intellectual Network." *Journal of British Studies* 4 (1964): 65–88.

Clapinson, Mary. Letter to the author, October 5, 1984.

De Morgan, Sophia Frend. *Memoirs of Augustus De Morgan.* London, 1882.

———. *Threescore Years and Ten: Reminiscences of the Late . . . De Morgan.* Edited by Mary A. De Morgan. London, 1895.

Dickens, Charles. *The Letters of Charles Dickens: The Pilgrim Edition,* 5 vols. Edited by Madeline House, Graham Storey, and Kathleen Tillotson. Oxford: Clarendon, Vol. 3: 1974.

Dubbey, J. M. *The Mathematical Work of Charles Babbage.* Cambridge: Cambridge University Press, 1978.

Elwin, Malcolm. *Lord Byron's Family: Annabella, Ada, and Augusta, 1816–1824.* Edited by Peter Thomson, London: John Murray, 1975.

Fawcette, James. "Ada Tackles Software Bottleneck." *High Technology* 3 (1983): 49–54.

Fonblanque, Albany. *The Life and Labours of Albany Fonblanque.* Edited by Edward Barrington de Fonblanque. London, 1874.

Fox, Caroline. *Memories of Old Friends.* Edited by Horace N. Pym. 2d ed. Philadelphia, 1884.

Gardner, Martin. Ed. *The Annotated Snark.* New York: Simon & Schuster, 1962.

Garland, Martha McMackin. *Cambridge Before Darwin: The Ideal of a Liberal Education, 1800–1860.* Cambridge: Cambridge University Press, 1980.

Gridgeman, Norman T. "Charles Babbage." *Dictionary of Scientific Biography* 1:355–6.

Hayes, Robert M. "Panizzi and Babbage: A Speculation." *Journal of Library History* 20 (Spring 1985): 179–85.

Hobhouse, John Cam (Lord Broughton). *Recollections of a Long Life.* 6 vols. Edited by Lady Dorchester. London: John Murray, 1911.

Hobsbawm, E. J. *The Age of Revolution: Europe, 1789–1848.* London: Weidenfeld & Nicolson, 1962.

Hodges, Andrew. *Alan Turing: The Enigma.* New York: Simon and Schuster, 1983.

Huskey, Velma R., and Harry D. Huskey. "Lady Lovelace and Charles Babbage." *Annals of the History of Computing* 2 (1980): 229–329.

"Ada, Countess of Lovelace, and her Contribution to Computing." *Abacus* 1 (Winter 1984): 22–29.

Hyman, Anthony. *Charles Babbage: Pioneer of the Computer.* New York: Oxford, University Press, 1982.

Knight, Frida. *University Rebel: The Life of William Frend, 1757–1841.* London: Victor Gollancz, 1971.

Lee, Robert. "Of the Malignant or Cancerous Disease of the Uterus." *The Cyclopaedia of Practical Medicine.* Edited by John Forbes, Alexander Tweedie, John Conolly. Rev. edited by Robley Dunglison. Philadelphia, (1854).

Linney, Romulus. *Childe Byron, A Play in Two Acts.* Produced at Circle Rep Theater in New York, 1981.

Lovelace, Ada. Four Uncatalogued Letters to Richard Taylor, August 1843. St. Bride Printing Office, London.

———. The Lovelace-Byron Collection of Letters in the Bodeian Library, Oxford.

———. The Babbage Collection in the British Library, London.

———. "Notes." [See entry under Morrison].

Marchand, Leslie A., ed. *Byron's Letters and Journals.* 12 vols. London: John Murray, 1973–1982.

Martineau, Harriet. *Autobiography of Harriet Martineau.* Edited by Maria Weston Chapman. 2 vols. Boston, 1877.

McConnell, Frank D., ed. *Byron's Poetry: A Critical Edition.* New York: Norton, 1978.

McCracken, Daniel D. *ACM* [Association of Computing Machines] Forum 24 (July 1981): 475.

Merz, John Theodore. *History of European Scientific Thought in the 19th Century.* 4 vols. Gloucester, Mass.: Peter Smith, 1896; reprint, 1976.

Moore, Doris Langley. *Ada, Countess of Lovelace: Byron's Legitimate Daughter.* London: John Murray, 1977.

Morrell, Jack, and Arnold Thackray. *Gentlemen of Science: Early Years of The British Association for the Advancement of Science.* Oxford: Clarendon, 1981.

Morrison, Philip, and Emily Morrison, eds. *Charles Babbage and His Calculating Engines,* including *Passages from The Life of a Philosopher* and "Sketch of the Analytical Engine Invented by Charles Babbage by L. F. Menabrea," with "Notes Upon the Memoir by the Translator, Ada Augusta, Countess of Lovelace." New York: Dover, 1961.

———. Letter to the author, May 10, 1984.

Mosley, James. Letter to the author, July 25, 1984.

Nabokov, Vladimir. *Ada or Ardor: A Family Chronicle.* New York: McGraw-Hill, 1969.

Patterson, Elizabeth Chambers. "Mary Somerville." *British Journal for the History of Science* 4 (1969): 311–39.

———. *Mary Somerville and the Cultivation of Science, 1815–1840.* Boston: Martinus Nijhoff, 1983.

Perl, Teri. "The *Ladies Diary* or *Woman's Almanac*, 1704–1841." *Historica Mathematica* 6 (1979): 36–53.

Peterson, M. Jeanne. *The Medical Profession in Mid-Victorian London.* Berkeley: University of California Press, 1978.

Pycior, Helena M. "At the Intersection of Mathematics and Humor: Lewis Carroll's Alices and Symbolical Algebra." *Victorian Studies* 28 (Fall 1984): 149–70.

Randall, Brian, ed. "Analytical Engines." In *The Origins of Digital Computers: Selected Papers.* 3d ed. New York: Springer-Verlag, 1982.

Stein, Dorothy K. "Lady Lovelace's Notes: Technical Text and Cultural Context." *Victorian Studies* 28 (Autumn 1984): 33–67. This is chapter 3 of *Ada: A Life and a Legacy* (Cambridge: MIT Press, 1985).

Taylor, R., ed. *Taylor's Scientific Memoirs, Selected from Transactions of Foreign Academies of Science and Learned Societies, and from Foreign Journals.* London: R. and J. Taylor, 1943.

Tee, Garry John. "The Heritage of Charles Babbage in Australasia." *Annals of the History of Computing* 5 (1983): 45–59. Adapted from a lecture, May 13, 1981, at the Second Australasian Mathematics Convention, University of Sydney.

Times of London. Supplement (November 27, 1852), 1.

"Vestiges of the Natural History of Creation." *Edinburgh Review* 82 (July 1845): 1–85. [Review].

Wallis, Ruth, and Peter Wallis. "Female Philomaths." *Historica Mathematica* 7 (1980): 57–64.

Wegner, Peter. "Ada—The Poetic Connection." *ACM Forum* 24 (May 1981): 329.

Weld, C. R. *History of the Royal Society.* London, 1848.

Whewell, William. "On the Connection of the Physical Sciences." *Quarterly Review* 51 (1834): 54–68.

Williams, M. R. "The Difference Engines." *Computer Journal* (February 1, 1976), 82–89.

[INDEX]

92
LOVELACE

Baum, Joan, 1937-

The calculating
passion of Ada
Byron

$21•50

DATE		

1/87

© THE BAKER & TAYLOR CO.